10-Minute
Time Outs
for
Moms

GRACE FOX

HARVEST HOUSE PUBLISHERS

EUGENE, OREGON

Cover by Koechel Peterson & Associates, Inc., Minneapolis, Minnesota

10-MINUTE TIME OUTS FOR MOMS
Copyright © 2004 by Grace Fox
Published by Harvest House Publishers
Eugene, OR 97402
www.harvesthousepublishers.com

Library of Congress Cataloging-in-Publication Data
    Fox, Grace, 1958–
        10-minute time outs for moms / Grace Fox.
            p. cm.
    Includes bibliographical references.
        ISBN 0-7369-1129-4 (pbk.)
    1. Mothers—Prayer-books and devotions—English. I. Title. Ten-minute time outs for moms. II. Title.
BV4847.F69 2004
242'.6431—dc22   2003015102

Printed in the United States of America

04 05 06 07 08 09 10 / DP-MS / 10 9 8 7 6 5 4 3

Acknowledgments

A huge thanks...

...to my husband and best friend, Gene, whose love, prayers, and computer savvy helped make this book a reality. I love you!

...to my teenagers—Matthew, Stephanie, and Kim—whose lives bless me every day. I'm privileged to be your mom!

...to my friends near and far, whose faithful prayers and encouragement have meant more than words can say.

...to my agent, Les Stobbe, for showing this manuscript to Barb Sherrill at Harvest House Publishers.

...and to my editor, Gene Skinner, whose skill and enthusiasm transformed my manuscript into *10-Minute Time Outs for Moms.*

Blessings, all!

A Note from the Author

Dear Moms,

I grew up loving babies and anticipating motherhood—nurturing wee polished cherubs, gathering them 'round for their favorite stories, savoring their sweet bedtime kisses.

In time, I bore a son and two daughters, but I hadn't anticipated the nauseous waves, the I'm-going-to-die-if-I-don't-eat-wonton-soup-right-now cravings, and the profile that resembled a swallowed beach ball. Then came labor and nighttime feedings and colic and chicken pox...need I say more?

When our third child arrived less than four years after the first, I admitted that motherhood involved more than I'd anticipated. With three unique, God-given gifts completely dependent on their dad and me, I felt overwhelmed. I discovered personality flaws I didn't know existed. I worried that my parenting imperfections might permanently scar my kids or leave their cherubs' wings lopsided, their haloes dented and scratched.

Do you ever feel like that?

If so, be encouraged: Moms aren't perfect, but God is. And because He's our perfect heavenly Father, He equips us for motherhood's monumental responsibilities. Everything we need, He supplies. Everything we lack, He is.

I took two decades and lots of life experience to figure this out, but I'm finally getting it right! Understanding God's character and applying that knowledge to my life has transformed my thinking and replaced fear with courage, worry with joy, dissatisfaction with contentment. Through life's ups and downs, I'm finding Him faithful, holy, wise, majestic, loving, consistent, and completely trustworthy. Focusing on His adequacies rather than my inadequacies brings confidence and security.

Perhaps you've already embraced these truths, and you're wondering what took me so long. (I'm asking myself the same thing!) May these devotionals refresh and encourage your spiritual journey.

Perhaps these truths are new to you. If that's the case, I pray that this book will lead you into an intimate and exciting relationship with the heavenly Father. May each day's "Upward Gaze" prayer and homespun story open new windows of understanding about God's character and how He relates to your everyday life.

I also hope you'll find confidence and power as you use the daily "Outward Glance" prayers for your children and other loved ones. Place their names in the blanks and claim the heavenly Father's promises on their behalf. You may find this prayer method especially encouraging when you simply don't know how to pray.

My prayer for you, and myself, is that our understanding of God's character will deepen and our lives will reflect a truth spoken by Mother Teresa: "Loving trust means an absolute, unconditional, and unwavering confidence in God our loving Father, even when everything seems to be a total failure; to look to Him alone as our help and protector, trusting to the point of rashness with courageous confidence in his fatherly goodness."

So, dear moms, find a quiet corner for your ten-minute timeout. May you return to your daily responsibilities refreshed and encouraged, assured that you're not alone in your task.

Know you are loved (thanks, Donna, for letting me borrow your line),

Grace

The Measureless Sea

The LORD loves righteousness and justice;
the earth is full of his unfailing love.
PSALM 33:5

Upward Gaze

I praise You today for Your goodness and unfailing love (1 Chronicles 16:34). Your love reaches to the heavens, Your faithfulness to the skies! (Psalm 36:5). My heart rejoices in Your salvation. You've been good to me, and I sing praises to Your name (Psalm 13:5-6). Your goodness to me can't be measured. Amen.

MOM

Every Sunday morning, three or four dozen children swarmed our church's basement, eager to hear Bible stories and sing songs—or at least hang out with their buddies. Freckle-faced boys greeted each other with a bop in the arm while pony-tailed girls giggled with their friends.

Chatter and laughter stopped at ten o'clock sharp when the Sunday school superintendent took her place behind a lectern. She introduced visitors, led us in singing "Happy Birthday," and collected a missionary offering. Then came the best part—singing action choruses.

We pretended to march in the Lord's army. We imitated Zaccheus climbing the tree to see Jesus. We sang about a fountain flowing deep and wide and about Jesus' love for all the children of the world. I enjoyed every tune, but my favorite song compared God's love to the ocean.

Growing up on Alberta's prairies limited my ocean knowledge to what I gleaned from television's *Voyage to the Bottom of the Sea*. But my ignorance didn't stop me from singing with gusto.

"Wide, wide as the ocean," I chirped, stretching my arms open from left to right, careful not to knock my neighbors' noses. "High as the heavens above"—I pointed skyward, imagining God's love reaching higher than fluffy white clouds. "Deep, deep as the deepest sea"—I pointed at the floor, visualizing His love extending to inky depths where submarines pinged and hid. I enjoyed singing and acting, but in reality, my limited imagination didn't comprehend the song's truth.

Thirty-five years and many life lessons later, I'm *finally* beginning to understand the height, depth, width, and consistency of God's measureless love. Living on an island surrounded by saltwater provides me with a perfect visual aid.

Each morning when I open the window blinds, I see the water. The tide rolls in and out, and the water level rises and falls, but it's always there. Local commercial fishermen count on it. Alaskan cruise companies sell tickets months in advance, believing it will always be there. Tugboat and barge owners book their business, banking on the sea's presence. And they're never disappointed.

Divers explore the sea's depths but will never exhaust its uncharted territory. It's simply too deep and too wide to conquer.

Like the ocean, God's love is wide, deep, and always there. We read about it in the Bible. We feel it in a child's hug. We see it in a friend's smile. It's with us throughout each day and while we sleep at night. It surrounds us when we're lonely and completely unaware of it. It embraces our children, and it will be there for their children, too. Even if, heaven forbid, the ocean should dry up someday, God's love will never run dry.

This knowledge fills our hearts with a confident song! In every circumstance, we can celebrate His measureless love.

Inward Glimpse

Heavenly Father, thank You for Your constant love. Help me face the future with confidence, knowing that Your love will always be with me. Amen.

- Record how God has shown His never-ending, unconditional love for you in the last week.
- In a sentence or two, thank God for His measureless love for you.

Outward Glance

Dear Father, thank You for Your unfailing love toward _____ (Psalm 6:4). Help him understand that love and never doubt it. May he fear You and hope in Your unfailing love. And as he does so, may Your eyes be on him (Psalm 33:18). Make him like the sun rising in its strength as he loves You (Judges 5:31). Amen.

One More Peek

For as high as the heavens are above the earth,
so great is his love for those who fear him
(Psalm 103:11).

This Place Is for You

Because you are sons, God sent the Spirit of his Son into our hearts,
the Spirit who calls out, "Abba, Father."
GALATIANS 4:6

Upward Gaze

Dear Father, I trust in Your unfailing love. I know You're with me every moment of every day. As I walk with You, nothing can change or remove Your love for me. My heart rejoices in Your salvation. I'll sing to You because of Your goodness to me (Psalm 13:5-6). I praise You for being my Abba Father and pouring Your love out upon me. Praise be to Your name, from everlasting to everlasting (1 Chronicles 16:36). Amen.

MOM

When I was young, visiting Grandma and Grandpa's farm was the next best thing to Christmas. I relished unlimited freedom and ran forever without fear of strangers or getting lost. Each visit brought wholesome adventures—discovering newborn kittens tucked between stacked hay bales, spying on piglets squeezed in a row against their monstrous mom, snuggling under Grandma's homemade feather comforter, and sneaking eggs from cackling hens. And Grandpa—well, he was better than any adventure.

"Come here, Gracie," he'd say, patting his knee. "This place is just for you."

I would run to him and climb onto his lap. He wrapped his strong arms around me and laughed his jolly laugh. I braced myself for the inevitable. Squeezing me so I couldn't escape, Grandpa put his cheek against mine and rubbed gently. Two days' whisker growth scratched my skin.

"Stop, Grandpa, stop!" I begged through my giggles. I squirmed to escape the sandpaper rub, careful that my wiggles weren't strong enough to free me. I loved every minute of his undivided attention. I felt like the safest, most-loved girl on earth. My heart sang, *Grandpa loves me, and I'm his girl!*

My Grandpa's love portrays God's Abba-love, His father-love, for His children. His arms are always open—"Come here, My child. This place is just for you." He delights when we crawl into His lap, leaving anxieties and fears behind. Nothing can touch us when we're safe in His arms.

Many women haven't known the love of a father or grandfather. Perhaps you find difficulty relating to Abba-love because of abuse suffered at the hands of those you trusted. If so, I pray that God, our heavenly Father, will show His love to you in special ways. I pray that He will heal your wounded heart and set you free to rejoice in the marvel of being His precious child.

Crawl onto His lap. Tell Him your concerns, fears, and joys. Ask Him for help with whatever you're facing today. Let Him wrap His arms around you. Close to the Father's heart, you're safe. Be still. Listen. Do you hear His voice?

I love you—you're My girl!

Inward Glimpse

Heavenly Father, thank You for claiming me as Your child through the blood of Jesus Christ. Take me by the hand and lead me into a greater understanding of the depth of Your love. Amen.

- Is anything in your life preventing you from enjoying God's Abba-love for you? If so, what is it? Ask God to remove any barrier and reveal His incredible love for you.
- Write a short prayer to acknowledge God's love for you. Begin with, "Daddy, thank You for loving me. I feel Your love when…"

Outward Glance

Father, I pray that _____ will know and love You as "Abba Father." May he keep Your commands, in order that he might receive Your promise to keep Your covenant of love to a thousand generations (Deuteronomy 7:9). I pray that he will trust in You as David did and that your unfailing love will hold him tightly, keeping him from being shaken (Psalm 21:7). Wrap Your loving arms around him today, I pray. Amen.

One More Peek

You did not receive a spirit that makes you a slave again to fear, but you received the Spirit of sonship. And by him we cry, "Abba, Father." The Spirit himself testifies with our spirit that we are God's children (Romans 8:14-16).

Goin' Fishin'

If the LORD delights in a man's way, he makes his steps firm;
though he stumble, he will not fall,
for the LORD upholds him with his hand.
PSALM 37:23-24

Upward Gaze

Father God, You are my refuge and my fortress, my God, in whom I trust. You save me from danger. You cover me with Your feathers and give refuge under Your wings. Your faithfulness is a shield and rampart. I will not fear the terror by night nor the arrow by day, nor pestilence, nor plague. A thousand may fall at my side, ten thousand at my right hand, but it will not come near me, for You, O God, surround me (Psalm 91:2-7). Amen.

MOM

One of my favorite little people lives next door. Five-year-old Colin provides entertainment money can't buy. His life tells more tales than a 40-year-old's does.

One day when Colin was only two years old, his mom, Rita, and I sipped coffee while he played a few feet away. "You'll never believe what he did this time," Rita said, leaning across the end table toward me and dropping her voice to a whisper.

"I can hardly wait," I said, chuckling at the thought of another of Colin's adventures. Rita's expression, however, warned me that this was serious.

"He opened the back door and ran away while I was talking on the phone," she said. "When I realized he was gone, his brothers and I looked everywhere. He wasn't in the yard or on the road. Finally his dad came home and joined the search. Guess where he found him?" Rita looked at me, waiting for an answer.

Endless hiding places surround us. Our homes hug a rocky shore beside a saltwater harbor. Forests encircle the camp property. If Colin had wandered alone outside his yard's safe confines, he could have gone anywhere.

"By the water?" I asked, hoping I was wrong.

Rita nodded slowly. "His dad found him walking toward the camp wharf with a fishing rod slung over his shoulder. When Colin saw him, he said, 'I'm goin' fishin', Dad!' He had no concept of being in danger."

I let out a slow breath. The wharf juts 450 feet into the harbor. Frigid water lies beneath it, covering huge boulders at high tide, exposing them at low tide. Wooden railings line the wharf for safety, but a small child could easily step between them and plunge to the icy water or rocks below. Chills rippled through my body. I watched Colin grab a toy tractor and *vvrroom* across the carpet, thankful that God had protected him.

As I relayed the story to Gene later that evening, I thought of how God, in His mercy, protects us. Sometimes we charge headlong into new experiences without asking for His direction first. We mean no harm, but excitement replaces common sense. Before long, we've overcommitted our time or resources, enthusiasm dies, and we wonder how in the world we'll survive.

Sometimes God rescues us through a Bible verse that leaps off the page. Sometimes He uses a gentle nudge, a quiet voice saying, "This isn't where I want you to be. Stay away from it." Perhaps it's a proposed business partnership. Maybe it's a personal relationship or a job offer. Sometimes all the circumstances seem to fit just right, but a nagging uneasiness in our spirit says otherwise.

God is faithful to keep us on the right track when our hearts are open to His ways. And His ways are always best.

Inward Glimpse

Dear Father, thank You for protecting me. Keep my heart open to Your voice and willing to follow Your leading. Amen.

- Recall a time when God protected you from a potentially dangerous situation.
- Memorize Psalm 16:7-9.

Outward Glance

Father, I pray that You will command Your angels to guard _____ in all her ways. May she love and acknowledge Your name, and as she does so, please rescue and protect her. Answer her when she calls on You. Be with her in trouble. Deliver and honor her. Show her Your salvation and satisfy her with a long life (Psalm 91:11,14-16). Keep her as the apple of Your eye and hide her in the shadow of Your wings (Psalm 17:8). Amen.

One More Peek

The righteous will inherit the land
and dwell in it forever.
The mouth of the righteous man utters wisdom,
and his tongue speaks what is just.
The law of his God is in his heart;
his feet do not slip (Psalm 37:29-31).

Follow the Leader

It is the LORD your God you must follow, and him you must revere.
Keep his commands and obey him; serve him and hold fast to him.
DEUTERONOMY 13:4

Upward Gaze

Heavenly Father, I praise You because You lead me beside still waters and guide me in paths of righteousness for Your name's sake (Psalm 23:2-3). I will follow You because You are my strength and shield. My heart trusts in You, and I am helped. My heart leaps for joy, and I will give thanks to You in song (Psalm 28:7). Amen.

MOM

Rrrrring! The recess bell clanged and clattered, and the school doors flew open. Eager elementary-aged students streamed onto the playground. Some kids swarmed around the slides, swings, and merry-go-round. Others played group games like follow-the-leader.

"I'll be the leader," announced Mandy.

"No fair. I want to be the leader," protested Jason, a freckled second-grader.

"You can do it next time," Mandy replied. "Follow me."

A half-dozen boys and girls formed a single line behind Mandy, and the game began. She somersaulted, they copied. She performed three jumping jacks, they imitated. She skipped across the school's empty baseball diamond, they followed. Several minutes later, she turned to Jason.

"Okay. Your turn."

Jason grinned. Like two flashing amber lights, his eyes twinkled *Mischief! Mischief!* He picked up a small rock and hurled it at the nearest window, missing the pane by mere inches.

The group gawked. "You can't do that!" exclaimed a classmate. "You'll get into trouble!"

"I'm not copying you," stated another. "I'd rather follow Mandy."

"If we follow you, we'll all end up at the principal's office," said a third. With that, the game ended. One by one, the kids abandoned Jason and returned to the school building.

Smart kids choose to follow a wise leader! Let's hope they remember the lesson as they enter their teen years.

Following the wrong leader isn't an innocent game when issues such as alcohol, illegal drugs, and premarital sex are involved. Peers, television, movies, radio, magazines—all urge our kids to copycat their values, pursue their path. Only a strong child or teen can say, "I'm not following you."

Even adults must decide whom they wish to mirror. On one hand, society coaxes, "Come my way. Earn more money. Drive a newer car. Buy a nicer house. Look out for number one—grab the leadership reins and follow your own desires."

On the other hand, the Bible teaches us to follow God's way. Avoid heartache. Invest in eternal matters. Be content. Practice servanthood.

Our emotions tempt us to do what feels best or what's most convenient. God's Word instructs otherwise. Deuteronomy 13:4 offers wise, straightforward counsel; Follow the Lord. Revere Him. Serve Him.

The Bible contains many accounts of men and women who followed God. Sometimes they risked their reputations. Sometimes they didn't understand what God was doing, but they chose to follow Him regardless. Moses is a prime example. He didn't understand how he could possibly lead the Israelites out of Egypt, but he followed God nonetheless (Exodus 3:4–4:31).

Think about Mary. She didn't understand how she could bear God's Son if she was still a virgin, but she followed anyway (Luke 1:29-38).

Peter, Andrew, James, and John set down their fishing nets and left their boats to respond to Jesus' invitation, "Follow me" (Matthew 4:18-22). Saul of Tarsus later joined their ranks as a Jesus follower (Acts 9:1-9).

Was the road easy? No. Was following Jesus worth the effort? Absolutely.

Is it worth it today? Again, absolutely. Only He leads us in paths of righteousness (Psalm 23:3). Only He knows what lies on the path ahead. Only He gives us the strength to do what we never thought possible.

Let's follow the leader—the true, all-wise Leader. Each time we choose to follow Him, in little and big issues alike, we win.

Inward Glimpse

Dear Father, You are the best Leader. Help me follow You in every decision of every day. Amen.

- Who are you sometimes tempted to follow? Society? Yourself? Write a prayer, committing yourself to following God's ways.
- How has God blessed you for following Him?

Outward Glance

Father, I pray that _____ will not follow the gods of the people around her. Instead, may she fear You and serve You only, obeying Your commands so it may go well with her (Deuteronomy 6:13-14,18). May she follow Your precepts and have good understanding (Psalm 111:10). Amen.

One More Peek

As they were walking along the road, a man said to him, "I will follow you wherever you go." Jesus replied, "Foxes have holes and birds of the air have nests, but the Son of Man has no place to lay his head" (Luke 9:57-58).

David and the Giant

Do not be fainthearted or afraid; do not be terrified or give way to panic before them. For the LORD your God is the one who goes with you to fight for you against your enemies to give you victory.
DEUTERONOMY 20:3-4

Upward Gaze

Father God, I offer my praise today because You fight the battles for me (1 Samuel 17:47). You act on my behalf, and nothing can hinder You from saving (1 Samuel 14:6). Some may trust in chariots and some in horses, but I will trust in Your name because You are the Lord God, and above You is no other (Psalm 20:7). Amen.

Children often put adults to shame with their amazing understanding of spiritual truth. Take David, for example. He was a simple shepherd boy, but his understanding of God's character outshone the faith of a king and thousands of Israelite warriors.

When David wandered onto the scene, the Israelites and the Philistines were camped opposite each other with a valley between them. The battle was at a stalemate. Suddenly Goliath stomped in, just as he did every morning and evening.

"Who's brave enough to face me?" Goliath bellowed. The Israelites ran for cover as usual. All except for David, that is. He wasn't stupid or frozen in fear. He understood the danger, all right. But he couldn't understand why the danger intimidated the army. After all, wasn't God the Commander in Chief? And if the living God was in charge, why would everyone be terrified of a measly giant?

King Saul shook his head at the youth's innocent confidence. "Open your eyes, little guy," he answered. "Goliath's been a warrior for years. You're just a kid. You don't stand a chance."

The boy couldn't be distracted. "With all due respect, King, you don't understand," David persisted. "I've killed lions and bears! Just as the living God delivered me from the hand of the wild animals, He'll deliver me from the giant as well."

Yeah, right, thought King Saul. Then he answered, "If you insist, I'll lend you my armor for protection." Saul hung his gear on the boy, but it did no good. David couldn't move.

"I don't need this stuff," declared David, removing the oversized armor. "God will deliver me from Goliath." He marched outside and picked up five smooth stones. Turning to face the snorting bully, he announced, "Hey you! Your weapons are toys compared to what I have!" Then he added, "God's the Boss, and He's on my side! Say goodnight!" He ran toward Goliath, took aim, and fired.

The stone found its target. Goliath slumped to the ground, defeated. A child's faith delivered an army from paralyzing fear! A child's focus delivered his people from powerless fright!

How could this be? With childlike faith, David took God at His word. He understood God's power. He knew God fought the battle for him. He claimed the victory because he knew God could not be defeated.

David's faith challenges us. We face Goliaths, too, but not always with the confident assurance David displayed. Our knees knock when we face giants such as *What will people think of me if I tell them I'm a Christian? What did the doctor say—cancer? Why must we move when our kids are doing so well in their school and all our friends are here?*

Like Saul placing his armor on David, we often try to fight our battles with a human approach. But our approach often doesn't work. Goliath's taunts intimidate us, and we end up worried or frightened.

David's simple faith sets our perspective straight. We don't fight our battles alone! With our focus on the living, all-powerful God, who can even raise the dead, we're guaranteed victory.

Inward Glimpse

Almighty God, I praise You for Your awesome power. I'm thankful You're on my side. Help me keep my focus on You rather than on circumstances. Amen.

- What are the Goliaths in your life? Where is your focus? Write a prayer to God, praising Him for fighting the battle for you.
- Read and enjoy the poem "Goliath" on the next page. I wrote this after I'd been deeply wounded by someone I'd considered a close friend. My Goliath was fear—the fear of seeing her and not knowing how to respond. God graciously reminded me that He was bigger than my Goliath and that He would lead me to victory if I relied on Him. I pray that the words will encourage you as you face Goliath today.

Outward Glance

Heavenly Father, I pray You will answer _____ when he's in distress. May Your name protect him. I trust You to rescue him with the saving power of Your right hand. While those who trust in human effort are brought to their knees, may he rise up and stand firm (Psalm 20:1,6,8). Amen.

One More Peek

This is what the LORD *says to you: "Do not be afraid or discouraged because of this vast army. For the battle is not yours, but God's"* (2 Chronicles 20:15).

Goliath

Grace Fox

Goliath might seem big and strong,
But his existence won't be long.
When you call on the living God,
He fights, He wins, and nations stand to applaud!

Admit to God you're terrified;
He'll stand up for you, He's on your side.
The nature of the battle says it's true—
His extraordinary power works for you!

Where does your focus lie?
Are you looking at Goliath or the God whom he defies?
Where does your focus lie?
How will God be glorified if you're looking at Goliath and
    believing Satan's lies?
Where does your focus lie?

Don't fall for the lies when the odds are overwhelming,
Don't fall for the lies when the stats are looking grim.
Believe the truth, don't fall for the lies,
Courage and victory come from Him!

Bus Ride

As I was with Moses, so I will be with you;
I will never leave you nor forsake you.
JOSHUA 1:5

Upward Gaze

Father, I praise You for Your omnipresence. Heaven is Your throne, and the earth is Your footstool (Isaiah 66:1). You are a God who is nearby and far away, filling heaven and earth (Jeremiah 23:24). Your Spirit is everywhere—in the heavens, in the depths. I can rise on the wings of the dawn and settle on the far side of the sea—You're there (Psalm 139:9). Amen.

MOM

The old Nepalese bus idled in the muddy parking lot, rattling and choking on its own diesel fumes. Baby-toting women wrapped in red saris boarded the vehicle while men wrestled with ornery goats objecting to riding on its roof.

I gawked at the goings-on and groaned. *Do we have to ride the bus? Is this our only choice?*

We'd been studying the language in Kathmandu since arriving in Nepal three months earlier. The time had arrived to find suitable housing in the district where Gene would soon work on a hydroelectric power project and I would teach basic health care. This was our only mode of transportation for the 12-hour trip.

The bus driver blasted the horn and revved the motor. Gene and I scrunched into a seat against the rear window. Three Nepalese shared our space. My head throbbed. My morning-sickness nausea doubled and then quadrupled.

The vehicle lurched and spewed black smoke as it wound its way through city streets. Finally it reached the hills surrounding Kathmandu Valley. The narrow road snaked along terraced hillsides at dizzying heights. The valley's floor lay thousands of feet below. When oncoming buses or transport trucks approached, our driver casually swung the bus nearer the road's edge to pass safely. Nothing had prepared me for this, least of all my growing-up years on Alberta's flat prairies. I'd never been so scared, and my head—I'd never felt such pain.

Every teetering curve dashed my thoughts deeper into dangerous territory. *I'm gonna die out here. If the bus ride doesn't kill me, the brain tumor will. Brain tumor? What brain tumor? Of course I have a tumor— what else could cause so much pain?*

Before long I'd planned my funeral and was wondering who Gene would marry after I was gone. Self-pity and fear swirled together like nasty chemicals in a botched high-school lab experiment. An explosion was imminent!

I don't know what shook me into reality, but suddenly I realized my desperate mental and emotional state. *Get a grip!* I reprimanded myself. *You don't have a tumor—it's probably a sinus infection. And did it ever occur to you that prayer might be appropriate right now?*

Oh yeah, I thought. *When all else fails…*

And so I prayed. *Keep this bus on the road! Don't let it tumble over the edge! Guard us from a head-on collision!* It wasn't working. My panicked pleas only intensified anxiety.

With sheer willpower, I changed my approach. *Thank You, God, for being with us right now. Thanks for promising never to leave us. You know exactly where we are; Your eyes are on us, and Your presence is with us.* I imagined God sitting between Gene and me, His arms around our shoulders. Peace gradually replaced fear as I conversed with God from that back seat. My thoughts calmed, enabling me to see our situation from a new perspective.

The bus continued to rock and rumble around hairpin curves, but I relaxed. I noticed farmers tending their fields and children toting huge loads of firewood on their backs. I noticed our fellow passengers' fearful expressions, and I felt compassion. I remembered that these people were the reason we had come to this land.

Life twists and turns just like that road. We can imagine the worst and hang on for dear life, or we can take a deep breath and praise God for His presence and power. Praising Him changes our perspective. It remedies panic and restores peace. And as our outlook changes, we become less focused on personal needs. We become more aware of those around us.

It doesn't stop there, for as our lives reflect hope and joy to those around us, others will thirst for the same thing. Through our living example and spoken word, we'll enjoy opportunities to tell others about Jesus Christ, whose sacrifice enables us to enjoy God's presence in our lives.

Inward Glimpse

Heavenly Father, thank You for Your presence every moment of every day. When the road twists unexpectedly, please remind me that You're near! Thank You. Amen.

- Do you sometimes wonder where God is? Write today's key verse on a recipe card and put it on your fridge.
- Together with your children, memorize the key verse and talk about its truth at meal times, while driving in the car, or going for a walk.

Outward Glance

Father, just as Your presence went with men like Moses, David, Solomon, and Job, I pray that you will walk with __ _____. Turn his heart to You, that he might walk in Your ways and keep Your commandments. Answer my prayer,

Lord, that the peoples of the earth may know that You are God and there is no other (1 Kings 8:57-60). Amen.

One More Peek

Keep your lives free from the love of money and be content with what you have, because God has said, "Never will I leave you; never will I forsake you." So we say with confidence, "The Lord is my helper; I will not be afraid. What can man do to me?" (Hebrews 13:5-6).

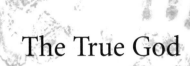

The True God

I am the LORD; that is my name!
I will not give my glory to another
or my praise to idols.
ISAIAH 42:8

Upward Gaze

Heavenly Father, I declare Your glory among the nations, Your marvelous deeds among all peoples. You are great and worthy of praise; You're to be feared above all gods. All the nations' gods are idols, but You made the heavens. Splendor and majesty are before You; strength and joy are in Your dwelling place (1 Chronicles 16:24-27). Amen.

◄ MOM ►

The sight stunned me. All my life I'd heard about idol worship. But living in Kathmandu, a city that boasts more idols than inhabitants, I witnessed it firsthand.

A dirty-faced girl, maybe six or seven years old, knelt before a three-foot-high chipped gray stone. She placed a yellow flower at its base and dabbed red powder on its face. Worship complete, she dodged a free-roaming cow wearing a marigold lei and dashed home.

On the next block, men and women entered a dank, dark temple adorned with flapping red, yellow, white, and green prayer flags. Inside, a pot-bellied bronze Buddha sat cross-legged, oblivious to the rice, grain, and floral offerings at its feet.

Watching the people's religious routines broke my heart. *They've placed their faith in deaf, dumb, mute god imitations,* I thought. *Gods that offer no answers, no salvation, no hope.*

I recalled an Old Testament story I'd heard as a child. It told of Israel's idol worship and how God's appointed servant, Elijah, confronted it.

"If the Lord is God, follow him. But if Baal is God, follow him," boomed Elijah to the crowd and 450 prophets of Baal. He proposed a plan to prove his point: He and Baal's prophets would build two altars and prepare two sacrificial bulls. Rather than light fires, however, they would ask their gods for flames.

Baal's followers went first. From early morning until noon they danced and shouted, "Baal, answer us!" No response.

Elijah watched in silence until he couldn't restrain himself. "Shout louder," he taunted. "Maybe he's thinking about other things! Maybe he's on vacation, or busy, or sleeping!"

The men yelled louder, cutting themselves with swords and spears. The afternoon passed. Evening approached. Still there was no response.

Elijah stepped forward. Silence swept through the crowd as he prepared his altar and commanded that it be flooded with water. Then he prayed. "Answer me, O Lord, so these people will know that you, the Lord, are God."

Boom! Heaven's fire fell, consuming not only the sacrifice but also the wood, the stone altar, the surrounding soil, and the water. Men, women, and children dropped on their faces crying, "The LORD—he is God! The LORD—he is God!" (1 Kings 18:39).

Baal, the lifeless idol, lost the battle to the true living God.

Scripture describes idols in a sarcastic, almost humorous manner. Isaiah says a carpenter grows trees, then cuts them down. He uses half the wood for a warming fire or cooking fuel. With the other half, he carves a god to which he prays, "Save me; you are my god" (Isaiah 44:16-17). He's asking an impossible request from a lifeless object.

The Psalmist writes that idols lack breath. They have mouths but can't speak, eyes but can't see, ears but can't hear (Psalm 135:16-17). On the other hand, God is very much alive. Psalm 34:15 says, "The eyes of the LORD are on the righteous and his ears are attentive to their cry."

Psalm 33:6 proves He has breath and that His mouth speaks: "By the word of the LORD were the heavens made, their starry host by the breath of his mouth."

The Bible says God sees us, hears our prayers, speaks with authority, and breathes life into His creation. This powerful, living God dwells within us by His Holy Spirit. He gives us eternal life, and someday He'll take us to heaven to spend eternity with Him. Wow!

This knowledge lends joy and confidence, peace and hope. We're loved and cared for by this very much alive God, who dwells everywhere at once and deserves our worship!

Inward Glimpse

Father, thank You that Your ears and eyes are open to me. Help me be faithful to You and not be swept into idol worship of any sort. Amen.

- Does God have your full affection? What idols might you be tempted to worship?
- Write a prayer that asks God to keep your heart true to Him alone.

Outward Glance

Father, I pray that _____ will realize the folly of idols. Teach her wisdom in these matters. Grant her discernment that she might understand them. May she walk in Your ways, for they are right (Hosea 14:9). Amen.

One More Peek

Elijah went before the people and said, "How long will you waver between two opinions? If the LORD is God, follow him; but if Baal is God, follow him" (1 Kings 18:21).

Mighty Miracles

Look to the LORD and his strength; seek his face always.
Remember the wonders he has done, his miracles,
and the judgments he pronounced.
1 CHRONICLES 16:11-12

Upward Gaze

Father God, You're the hope of all the ends of the earth
and of the farthest seas. You formed the mountains by Your
power, having armed Yourself with strength. You stilled the
roaring seas and the nations' turmoil. People fear Your
wonders. Where morning dawns and evening fades, You call
forth songs of joy (Psalm 65:5-8). Amen.

MOM

I'll never forget the doctor's words: "Stephanie will die within a
month." He explained that besides suffering from hydrocephalus—too
much fluid on her brain—she was also born with ventricular septal
defect, a serious heart problem. "If she lives until she's two years old,
we can perform open-heart surgery," he said. "When babies are this sick,
however, they usually don't survive that long."

I stood beside Stephanie's isolette in Tacoma General's neonatal intensive care unit. Tape and tubes covered her tiny frame. Only two weeks
old, she'd already undergone surgery to reduce pressure on her brain.

"You can take her home now, but bring her back when her heart
begins to fail," he continued. "She'll die here." He paused and then added,
"I'm sorry."

The room reeled. Questions swirled through my mind as I studied my sleeping daughter. *My baby—die in a month? How could this be happening? Should we seek a second opinion?*

That evening I relayed the doctor's prognosis to Gene. Together we prayed for Stephanie's healing. We activated church prayer chains. We composed a letter for friends worldwide explaining the situation and requesting prayer on her behalf.

Two months later, the same doctor examined her. He slapped her x-rays onto the light screen, stroked his chin, and stared in silence. Finally he spoke. "I don't believe it. Her heart is normal."

Gene and I grinned. We believed it. God performed a miracle—there was no other explanation. Even the medical doctor had to agree.

God does that sometimes. Why He doesn't do it all the time, I don't understand. The Bible says His ways aren't our ways. Stories don't always end the way we would like. Especially in those times, He asks us to trust.

But the fact remains—He is able to perform miracles. God's Word lists numerous accounts: In the Old Testament, He created the entire universe with a spoken word. He orchestrated the Egyptian plagues. He parted the Red Sea, allowing the Israelites to pass through on dry ground. He fed and clothed them for 40 years in the wilderness. He parted the Jordan River. Through Elijah and Elisha, he breathed life into two little boys' dead bodies. And that's just scratching the surface!

The New Testament records other instances: Jesus' mother was a virgin. As an adult, Jesus turned water into wine at a wedding. He healed the blind and the lame and raised the dead. He fed thousands with the contents of a young boy's sack lunch, calmed a raging storm with a verbal command, and walked through angry mobs unseen. In fact, John 21:25 says that Jesus did so many other things that if every one was written, the whole world couldn't contain the books.

But the greatest miracle of all was His resurrection from the dead. Three days after friends sealed His body in a cave-like tomb, the massive stone guarding the door was rolled away. His grave clothes lay neatly folded where His body had been placed. He wouldn't need them any longer—He had risen!

That miracle birthed another—eternal life for all who place their saving faith in Him. And when we've placed our saving faith in Christ, the Holy Spirit lives in us and will fill us with joy and peace and hope in every circumstance. And that's a miracle, too—one I pray for you!

Inward Glimpse

Heavenly Father, thank You for the miracles You perform on my behalf. Help me remember You're capable of doing the inexplicable. Amen.

- Have you witnessed a miracle in your life or the life of a loved one? If so, describe it.
- Write a prayer of praise to God for His ability to do the impossible. Ask Him for faith to believe Him for great things.

Outward Glance

Father, I pray that _____ will remember Your miracles of long ago. Teach her to meditate on all Your works and consider all Your mighty deeds. Show her that You are the God who performs miracles and displays Your power among the people (Psalm 77:11-14). Amen.

One More Peek

When Elisha reached the house, there was the boy lying dead on his couch. He went in, shut the door on the two of them and prayed to the Lord. Then he got on the bed and lay upon the boy, mouth to mouth, eyes to eyes, hands to hands. As he stretched himself out upon him, the boy's body grew warm (2 Kings 4:32-34).

The Great Provider

*And my God will meet all your needs
according to his glorious riches in Christ Jesus.*
PHILIPPIANS 4:19

Upward Gaze

You are worthy of praise, O God, for You are a sun and shield. You bestow favor and honor; You withhold no good thing from those whose walk is blameless (Psalm 84:11). Like a good shepherd, You know my needs and provide what's best for me. I rest in You, knowing that You're looking after me with tender, loving care (Psalm 23:1-5). Amen.

MOM

"We have no health insurance," Gene explained as we sat in the neonatal intensive care unit beside our daughter's isolette. "Our mission disposed of their health insurance a couple of months ago. They thought they could sell their real estate if their people had major needs." He shook his head. "No one thought this would happen."

Silence hung heavy in the room as we struggled to comprehend the situation's seriousness. Stephanie was only a few days old. Born with hydrocephalus, she required immediate neurosurgery to lessen the chances of serious brain damage. With treatment unavailable in Nepal, our only option was to return to the States.

Having lived on faith as missionaries for the previous three years, our bank account was minimal. Our sudden, unexpected departure from the field left us dangling—no job, no car, no home, and no insurance to pay mounting hospital bills for our critically ill baby.

"God is in control," Gene stated matter-of-factly. "He knows our need and will provide." Together we bowed our heads and confessed our absolute dependence on the Lord.

Two days later, we found a note attached to Stephanie's hospital bed. "If you require financial assistance," I read aloud, "fill out this form and contact the Washington State Crippled Children's Services."

We completed the questionnaire and submitted it. Within a few days we received notification of acceptance. The program paid her medical bills for a year, during which time she underwent five surgeries and a bout with meningitis.

Health insurance kicked in one month after the state program ended. During that month, she had no medical expenses—the first time since birth.

God provided for our needs in other ways, too. Gene found a civil engineering job two weeks after returning to the States. A stranger invited us to house-sit his furnished home. Several significant donations enabled us to buy a car. A loving church family surrounded us with prayer and practical support.

With such obvious evidences of His provisions, you might think I would never again worry or doubt when needs arise. I wish that were true, but I've tied myself in emotional knots over big expenses due at the same time—kid's orthodontic work, school band trips, blown head gaskets.

Each time I've stressed, God has gently reminded me to trust Him. After all, Scripture says He owns the cattle on a thousand hills—He certainly has the assets! And He sent Jesus to die for my sin so I could enjoy unbroken fellowship with Him. If He loves me to that extent, I can surely trust Him.

Indeed, we can trust Him. He may not always provide as we might choose. He might make us wait longer than we would prefer. He might answer with unexpected means. Sometimes He allows us the privilege of walking through lean times to experience the joy of contentment with little.

Whatever He does, it's His business—He's God, and He knows what He's doing. Our job is to trust.

Inward Glimpse

Father, You love me so much that You sent Your only Son to pay the penalty for my sin. Remind me of that love next time I worry about my situation. Amen.

- What are you trusting God to provide for you? Write a prayer to God and praise Him for His ability to provide. Express your desire to trust Him implicitly.

- Meditate on the hymn "'Tis So Sweet to Trust in Jesus" on the next page. What stanza means the most to you, and why?

Outward Glance

Father, thank You for faithfully providing for _____'s needs. Help her recognize her dependence on You for all things. And as surely as You provide her needs, may she give generously to others in need. May she prosper as she practices generosity, and be refreshed as she refreshes others (Proverbs 11:25). As she lends freely and conducts her affairs with justice, I pray that she'll never be shaken (Psalm 112:5-6). As she obeys, throw open the floodgates of heaven and pour out so much blessing that she won't have enough room for it (Malachi 3:10). Thank You, Father. Amen.

One More Peek

Remember the LORD your God, for it is he who gives you the ability to produce wealth, and so confirms his covenant, which he swore to your forefathers, as it is today (Deuteronomy 8:18).

'Tis So Sweet
to Trust in Jesus

Louisa M. R. Stead

'Tis so sweet to trust in Jesus,
  Just to take Him at His word;
Just to rest upon His promise;
  Just to know, "Thus saith the Lord."

O how sweet to trust in Jesus,
  Just to trust His cleansing blood;
Just in simple faith to plunge me
  'Neath the healing, cleansing flood!

Yes, 'tis sweet to trust in Jesus,
  Just from sin and self to cease;
Just from Jesus simply taking
  Life and rest, and joy and peace.

I'm so glad I learned to trust Thee,
  Precious Jesus, Savior, Friend;
And I know that Thou art with me,
  Wilt be with me to the end.

Jesus, Jesus, how I trust Him!
  How I've proved Him o'er and o'er!
Jesus, Jesus, precious Jesus!
  O for grace to trust Him more!

Sarah's Laughter

Is anything too hard for the LORD?
I will return to you at the appointed time next year
and Sarah will have a son.
GENESIS 18:14

Upward Gaze

O great and powerful God, You are the sovereign Lord.
You've made the heavens and earth by Your great power and
outstretched arm. Nothing is too hard for You (Jeremiah
32:17,27). Your plans can't be thwarted by anything or
anyone (Job 42:2). You are exalted above all else. I rest in
Your hands, knowing that You're in control. Amen.

Sarah's gasp changed to a snicker, grew to a giggle, and exploded
into full-blown laughter. She covered her mouth with a shawl, hoping
the sound wouldn't escape beyond the tent.

"Me?" she whispered, gasping for breath. "Pregnant?" She buried
her face in her shawl, stifling the erupting laughter. "That's the most
absurd thing I've ever heard!"

The old woman dropped to the floor, using a corner of her wrap
to wipe her eyes. What was it the stranger had said to her husband? "I
will surely return to you about this time next year, and Sarah your wife
will have a son."

Who does that guy think he is? Sarah wondered. *My biological clock quit ticking years ago. And Abraham's a wonderful husband, but he's not a young man anymore.* She shook her head. *We tried for years to have children. Isn't it a little late now?*

Outside the tent, muffled words crystallized as Abraham and the visitor approached the doorway. "Why did Sarah laugh at my words?" questioned the man. "Nothing's too hard for the Lord. I meant what I said. Sarah will become pregnant and have a son."

Sarah gasped once more, this time in fear. *Oh no! He heard me!* "I didn't laugh!" she shouted from inside the tent.

"Yes, you did." Sarah fell silent.

Nine months later she writhed in anguish. "Push!" cried the midwife. "One more push, and he'll be out!"

The old woman screamed in pain, the final excruciating effort sapping her last ounce of strength. The baby slid from her body's protection into the midwife's waiting arms.

Minutes later, gray-haired Sarah held her newborn to her breast. She stroked his satiny head as he sucked, half-asleep, unaware of the world around him. "A son!" she whispered. "*My* son!" Tears of joy flowed down her cheeks.

What was it the stranger had said? "Is anything too hard for the Lord?"

"He was right," she whispered to the baby. "Nothing, absolutely nothing is too difficult for the Lord—you are living proof."

When we feel overwhelmed with seemingly hopeless situations, we can remember Sarah and remind ourselves that God delights in doing the impossible. He has shown us His abilities through His Son, Jesus, who walked the earth as a man.

Jesus turned water into wine at a wedding reception. He healed the sick and restored sight to the blind. He fed thousands using a little boy's sack lunch. He walked on water and commanded a raging storm to be still.

His most amazing victory? He rose from the dead. By rolling away the stone that sealed His tomb and stepping into dawn, He defeated death and delivered the ultimate triumph. In doing so, He brought hope and victory for those who place their faith in Him.

Rather than falling into the unbelief trap, we can praise God for being bigger than our circumstances. When the odds are stacked against us, we can thank Him that nothing can thwart His purposes for our lives. If fear grips our heart in a difficult situation, we can meditate on the truth that nothing is impossible for God and be set free.

Inward Glimpse

Dear Father, thank You for reminding me that impossibilities are opportunities for You to prove Your omnipotence. You are bigger than any difficulty I will ever face. Help me focus on Your abilities rather than my doubts and fear. I pray in Jesus' name. Amen.

- What difficult circumstances are you facing? Write a prayer in which you commit those circumstances to God and recognize His ability to do the impossible.

- Recall a time when God worked out a seemingly impossible situation for you or someone else. He's the same God today as He was then!

Outward Glance

Father, I pray that _____ will view impossible situations as opportunities rather than roadblocks. May he focus on You when he encounters discouraging and frightening challenges. Teach him to believe that with You, all things are possible (Matthew 19:26). Show him Your power! Open his eyes and help him understand that according to Your great power at work within him, You're able to do immeasurably more than all he could ask or imagine (Ephesians 3:20). Amen.

One More Peek

Don't be alarmed....You are looking for Jesus the Nazarene, who was crucified. He has risen! He is not here. See the place where they laid him (Mark 16:6).

Thanks a Lot!

O LORD my God,
I will give you thanks forever.
PSALM 30:12

Upward Gaze

Heavenly Father, I praise You every day! I'll extol Your name forever because You are great and worthy of praise. No one can fathom Your greatness or mighty acts. Generations will speak of Your works to one another; they'll speak of Your glorious splendor and majesty. They'll tell of Your power and celebrate Your abundant goodness! (Psalm 145:1-7). Amen.

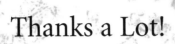

In his book *Who Put My Life on Fast-Forward?*[1] Phil Callaway writes that the truly successful life is hallmarked by an attitude of thanksgiving. He practices what he preaches even though the lesson hasn't been an easy one to learn.

Early in his marriage, his wife, Ramona, developed seizures. Her symptoms baffled doctors. For several years, her condition worsened until Phil feared she would die. In our recent phone conversation, he recalled tucking his four-year-old son into bed late after a Thanksgiving Day marred by numerous seizures.

"Jeffrey was having troubles sleeping that night," he said, "so I told him to think of a hundred things he was glad about. He looked up at me and said, 'Dad, you start.'"

Phil paused, the memory still vivid.

"Here I was, in the middle of the valley of the shadow of death, surrounded by doubts and fears and worries about tomorrow. I was wondering whether Ramona would still be alive when I returned to our bedroom. In the middle of that, I began to understand what the apostle Paul meant when he said, 'Rejoice in the Lord always. I will say it again: Rejoice!'"

It was my turn to be silent.

"You know what, Grace?" he asked. "We can *choose* thanksgiving in the midst of difficulty. Doing so completely changes a person. It not only transforms his faith, it transforms his face."

Phil's right. An attitude of gratitude changes a person from the inside out, removing seeds of bitterness and sowing seeds of righteousness. Those seeds blossom into joy and peace and the ability to smile in the face of difficulty and the unknown.

How do we practice thanksgiving, particularly when life stinks? By telling God, "Thanks for a new day, a fresh start, another chance to be surrounded by Your presence. Thanks for promising never to leave me. Thanks for holding me in Your hand. Thanks for the hope that Christ's resurrection brings. Thanks for an eternity filled with joy, where tears and pain and death don't exist!"

We practice thanksgiving by saying on a daily basis, "Thanks for sunshine and rain. Thanks for eyes to see creation's wonders—reminders of Your mighty strength. Thanks for ears to hear birds chirping praise to You for providing their needs. Thanks for legs to walk and arms to hold the beautiful children You've blessed me with."

Our example goes a long way in training our children. Developing an attitude of gratitude doesn't happen overnight, especially if negative habits have already been formed, but if we consistently express thanks to God and those around us for the things they do, we'll see changes in our kids, too.

Imagine our kids never grumbling when they're served cabbage rolls rather than chicken nuggets, but instead, recognizing the privilege of eating three meals a day. Never complaining about studying math and biology, but appreciating their educational opportunities. And never whining about making their beds or cleaning bathrooms, but being grateful for living in a house as opposed to a corrugated tin shanty somewhere in a Third World country.

A thankful heart understands who God is and recognizes His provision for our lives. A thankful heart attracts others to Christ through its contentment and joy, its ability to rejoice in the Lord in every circumstance.

May our faces reflect thankful hearts, and may our thankfulness reflect an understanding of God's presence and His countless blessings in our lives!

Inward Glimpse

Dear Father, thank You for life's countless blessings. Develop within me a thankful heart. Amen.

- List ten things for which you're thankful today.
- At mealtime, give each person an opportunity to say one thing he or she is thankful for today. Perhaps you could make this a daily routine.

Outward Glance

Heavenly Father, I pray that _____ will obey Your command to be joyful always, pray continually, and give thanks in all circumstances (1 Thessalonians 5:16-18). May he continuously give thanks and call on Your name. May he make known among the nations what You have done (Psalm 105:1). Amen.

One More Peek

Speak to one another with psalms, hymns and spiritual songs. Sing and make music in your heart to the Lord, always giving thanks to God the Father for everything, in the name of our Lord Jesus Christ (Ephesians 5:19-20).

Sentence or Servanthood?

Do everything without complaining or arguing.
PHILIPPIANS 2:14

Upward Gaze

In the midst of another busy day, I will enter Your gates with thanksgiving, God. I will enter Your courts with praise. I give thanks to You and praise Your name (Psalm 100:4). May You be exalted above the heavens. Let Your glory be over the whole earth! (Psalm 108:5). Amen.

It's true—moms spend a huge portion of their lives performing mundane tasks to serve others. Clothes cycle continuously from the dresser to the laundry hamper to the washing machine and back again. Dishes rotate from the cupboard to the table to the sink. Bathroom fixtures need wiping. Windows need washing. Floors need mopping.

Add other tasks such as grocery shopping, preparing meals, mending clothes, making dental or doctor appointments, planning birthday parties, chauffeuring kids to extra-curriculars, attending parent-teacher meetings, helping with homework, reading bedtime stories, and nursing sick children or elderly parents.

The list exhausts me! And it's far from complete, for some women work part-time or full-time outside their home. It's easy to slip into a mentality that says we're sentenced to the mundane.

According to Canadian statistics, 3.2 million women over the age of 15 spend between 5 and 14 hours per week doing unpaid housework.

That's not too bad. But what about almost 900,000 women who clean house 60 or more hours *per week?*

Whoa, baby, those houses must shine! Not a single dust mite, cat hair, or dust bunny lying around!

Now, consider unpaid childcare. Nearly 1.2 million Canadian women surveyed say they spend 60 or more hours per week caring for children, either their own or someone else's.

When our three children were under the age of four, cleaning and child care overwhelmed me at times. I stumbled through a phase when I thought my brain had turned to mush for lack of outside stimulation or adult conversation. Grumbling eroded my joy and peace. I envied my husband—he commuted 90 minutes a day, five days a week, to and from work. That equaled 450 minutes or 7.5 hours per week, doing nothing but enjoying time for himself!

When I expressed my jealousy, he stared at me in disbelief. "I'm not enjoying quiet," he exclaimed, "I'm fighting freeway traffic!"

Aahh—a nice change from scrubbing toilets and tripping over toys all day, I thought.

The phase eventually passed, thank goodness. Pursuing personal interests such as singing in the church choir helped me move beyond my "I'm just a slave" mentality.

But more importantly, I discovered an attitude-changing truth. Choices face us regardless of our role in life. As moms, we can regard meal preparation as monotonous and dirty laundry as drudgery, or we can consider them as evidences of God's physical provisions—food and clothing!

Dirty floors and toilets can become blessings in disguise. If we didn't have homes to clean, we'd be living on the street. Muddy footprints on freshly washed kitchen linoleum and sticky fingerprints on living room windows evidence active children in our homes. And another hour chauffeuring to music lessons means a child is developing a useful talent.

When we grow frustrated with our responsibility to serve others, we can find encouragement in Jesus Christ's example. Scripture says He washed His disciples' feet. Imagine! The almighty God-Man, to whom all praise and worship belongs, stooped over a basin and tenderly washed the dust from His followers' feet.

Our homemaking and parenting responsibilities provide great opportunities to display servant attitudes. Each task gives us a chance to kick off the "sentence" mentality and exemplify a Christlike servant's spirit. When we're tempted to grumble, we can choose to smile instead and treat our kids and spouse as though they were very special. After all, they are! Our children will learn positive attitudes towards service, and we'll be blessed for doing what's right.

Inward Glimpse

Dear Father, thank You for Christ's example of serving others without grumbling. Help me keep my heart free from complaining as I serve my family. Amen.

- Mother Teresa said, "The humbler the work, the greater should be your love and efficiency. Be not afraid of the life of sacrifice." Write this quote on a 3x5 card and put it by your kitchen sink.

- Read the "One More Peek" passage. When we grumble, who are we grumbling against?

Outward Glance

Father, I pray that _____ will follow Hezekiah's example and do what is good and right and faithful before You. May he seek You in everything he does. May he work wholeheartedly and prosper (2 Chronicles 31:20-21). As he works, I pray that he will do nothing from selfish ambition or conceit and that he'll consider others better than himself. May he take a servant's nature just as Christ did. May he do all things without complaining or grumbling (Philippians 2:3,7,14). I pray in Jesus' name. Amen.

One More Peek

Who are we, that you should grumble against us?...You will know that it was the LORD *when he gives you meat to eat in the evening and all the bread you want in the morning, because he has heard your grumbling against him. Who are we? You are not grumbling against us, but against the* LORD (Exodus 16:7-8).

Everywhere at Once

If I rise on the wings of the dawn,
if I settle on the far side of the sea,
even there your hand will guide me,
your right hand will hold me fast.
PSALM 139:9-10

Upward Gaze

Heavenly Father, You are the God of all places. You fill heaven and earth; no one can hide in secret from You (Jeremiah 23:23-24). Heaven is Your throne, and the earth is Your footstool (Isaiah 66:1). You hem me in behind and before and lay Your hand upon me. I can go nowhere to flee Your presence, for Your right hand will hold me wherever I am (Psalm 139:5-10). Amen.

MOM

I was having one of those days that makes a mom feel stretched beyond her capacity. You know the feeling—you're only one person, but you're pulled in several directions at once.

Sitting in a hospital room and cuddling Stephanie, I reviewed the three months since her birth. Countless doctor's appointments. Hospitalizations. Surgeries. I'd either dragged her two-year-old brother, Matthew, along or left him with a baby-sitter through each ordeal. Today his grandparents had offered to watch him.

Poor little guy, I thought. *Will he grow to resent our time spent with his little sister? Will he feel he is less loved than she is?* That was the last thing I wanted.

I looked at my watch and then at my sleeping baby. Stephanie's scheduled surgery was still several hours away. I had enough time to dash home and return before the anesthesiologist took her to the operating room. I tucked my daughter into her hospital crib and raced to my car for the 15-mile trip home.

"Mommy!" exclaimed Matthew when I stepped through the front door. "See?" He grinned and pointed at his construction masterpiece. Red, green, yellow, and blue building blocks surrounded him. Toy cars and trucks idled on plastic roads, waiting for a turn to visit a miniature parking garage.

Together we read a story or two. He showed me his morning's artwork and cuddled on my lap while I visited with his grandparents.

An hour later, I glanced at my watch again. *Oh dear—what if Stephanie wakes up before I return? What if the anesthesiologist arrives earlier than expected?* With that thought, I kissed Matthew goodbye and rushed back to the hospital.

I parked the car and then paused for a few moments as I gazed at Stephanie's third-floor window. *Lord, I'm tired. I just want to be home with my babies. They both need me, but I can't be in two places at once. Please watch over them. Thank You, Father.*

Minutes later I entered Stephanie's room. "Hi!" a cheerful voice rang. "I just *love* this baby!" My pastor's wife, Trish, walked toward me, holding Stephanie. The baby cooed and gurgled. "I hope you don't mind!"

I smiled. *Mind?* I had just prayed, *I can't be in two places at once. Please watch over my children.* God had answered. Matthew's grandparents cared for his needs. A loving friend cradled Stephanie.

Our heavenly Father loves our children far more than we can imagine. In His tender, omnipresent care, He watches over them. He's with our kids when they ride the school bus or attend their first sleepover. He's with them at summer camp, on the newspaper route, in their college dormitory, or in military service overseas.

Sometimes our children face injury or encounter evil—perhaps an abuser or the neighborhood bully. We wonder, *Where was God when my child needed Him?* That's a tough question. Sin makes our world a hurtful place, and unfortunately, innocent people often suffer from other people's wrongdoing.

In difficult times, we find encouragement in knowing that God understands our feelings. His Son bore the consequences of other people's sin when He died on the cross. And even Jesus felt abandoned when He cried, "God, why have you forsaken me?" But Jesus' victorious resurrection three days later chases away hopelessness and fear.

God's willingness to allow His Son to die on our children's behalf tells me that He loves them. We can trust Him with their care. We can give Him our concerns for our children's well-being, and we can thank Him for watching over them wherever they go.

Inward Glimpse

Dear Father, thank You for being with my children wherever they are, day or night. Surround them with a sense of Your presence. Amen.

- List the places your children spend time. Thank God for being with them in each of those places.
- Read the hymn "Under His Wings" on page 52. What does this song mean to You?

Outward Glance

Father, I pray that _____ will be strong and courageous wherever he goes. Remind him that You are with him wherever he is. Reassure him that You will never leave him or forsake him (Deuteronomy 31:6,8). Amen.

One More Peek

In my distress I called to the LORD, and he answered me. From the depths of the grave I called for help, and you listened to my cry (Jonah 2:2).

Under His Wings

William O. Cushing

Under His wings I am safely abiding;
Though the night deepens and tempests are wild,
Still I can trust Him; I know He will keep me;
He has redeemed me, and I am His child.

Under His wings, what a refuge in sorrow!
How the heart yearningly turns to His rest!
Often when earth has no balm for my healing,
There I find comfort, and there I am blest.

Under His wings, O what precious enjoyment!
There will I hide till life's trials are o'er;
Sheltered, protected, no evil can harm me;
Resting in Jesus, I'm safe evermore.

Under His wings, under His wings,
Who from His love can sever?
Under His wings my soul shall abide,
Safely abide forever.

My Watchman

Unless the LORD builds the house, its builders labor in vain.
Unless the LORD watches over the city,
the watchmen stand guard in vain.
PSALM 127:1

Upward Gaze

Father, I love You for hearing my cry for mercy. When I call out in time of trouble, You run to my rescue. You are full of grace, righteousness, and compassion. I will call on You as long as I live. My soul rests, for You have been good to me (Psalm 116:1-2,5,7). Amen.

My husband served as a volunteer firefighter and emergency medical technician in Lacey, Washington for about six years. In fact, we lived at a fire department substation on the city's outskirts. Our driveway, which we shared with the substation garage, sat on public property. Strangers occasionally knocked on our door to ask for directions or medical attention. Alone every day with three preschoolers, I sometimes felt vulnerable.

My fear grew after someone broke into our house in our absence. The thief took our camera and rifled through my dresser drawers, stealing several articles of jewelry, including a gold necklace Gene had given me on our wedding night. The robber was never caught.

When Gene's job began requiring frequent out-of-town business trips, apprehension stared me in the face. *What if a stranger knocks on the door in the night?* I worried. *What if the thief returns? How will I protect the children and myself?*

Attempting to alleviate fright, I turned on the nightstand lamp before going to bed. If something went *bump* in the night, I wanted to see who or what it was! Despite the light, wind and creaks woke me. Tires screeching on the nearby road scared me. Sleep evaded me for hours. I rose each morning exhausted and with barely enough energy to care for my kids.

One night I crawled into bed thinking, *I can't take this anymore! I'm in total bondage to fear. I'm a captive in my own home.* I longed for freedom from worry, for the ability to lie down and sleep in peace, enveloped by God's presence and protection.

In desperation, I opened my Bible to the Psalms. There I read, "Unless the LORD builds the house, they labor in vain who build it; unless the LORD guards the city, the watchman keeps awake in vain" (Psalm 127:1 NASB). The verse grabbed my attention. I read it again.

Suddenly the words seemed pointed and personal. Staying awake at night was useless because I wasn't the one guarding my home and children—God was! And He didn't need my help. I was free to sleep while God and His angels patrolled the yard and watched as sentries at the door.

The revelation released me. I continued using locks and an outdoor motion-detecting light, but I never again slept with the nightstand light on.

That verse's liberating truth affects every aspect of our lives. It not only removes fear, but it replaces stress with rest. It reassures us that God can manage our concerns.

In parenting, for instance, we can knock ourselves out trying to raise good kids. We can worry ourselves sick if they make poor choices. Or we can pray, be responsible moms, and trust the Holy Spirit to guide and teach them.

In other areas of life, we can pour hours into supervising church programs and feel disappointed and frustrated over lack of obvious results. Or we can pray, do our homework, and trust the Lord to build His programs His way.

The principle even applies to finances. We can run ourselves ragged, neglecting family and friends to work overtime, and still run out of money before the month ends. Or we can be responsible stewards and trust God to provide for our needs.

Rest or stress? Freedom or fear? The choice is ours. By God's grace, we can choose well and watch Him work on our behalf.

Inward Glimpse

Heavenly Father, thank You for giving me rest in the midst of stress. Help me remember that You are the builder and watchman over every area of my life. Amen.

- Are you facing a situation that frightens or stresses you? If so, what is it?
- Write a short prayer and invite God to take control over it.

Outward Glance

Heavenly Father, I pray that _____ will not place her faith in mortal men, who cannot save. May she seek You for help. May she place her hope completely in You, maker of heaven and earth, the sea, and everything in them. May she constantly turn to You because You remain faithful forever (Psalm 146:3,5-6). Amen.

One More Peek

He will not let your foot slip—
He who watches over you will not slumber;
indeed, he who watches over Israel
will neither slumber nor sleep....
The Lord will keep you from all harm—
he will watch over your life;
the Lord will watch over your coming and going
both now and forevermore (Psalm 121:3-4,7-8).

Grandma Made It

Now to the King eternal, immortal, invisible, the only God,
be honor and glory for ever and ever.
1 TIMOTHY 1:17

Upward Gaze

Invisible Father, I praise You for revealing Yourself through Jesus. All things were created by Him and for Him. Your fullness dwells in Him, and through Him You reconciled all things to Yourself (Colossians 1:15-20). I praise You for revealing Yourself through creation and man's conscience (Romans 1:18-20). Amen.

MOM

Our family vacationed in an out-of-the-way Washington seaside community when our children were preschoolers. The kids loved to collect sand dollars and build sand castles. They splashed in sun-warmed tidal pools and giggled when tiny crabs scurried across their bare feet.

One afternoon as we prepared for yet another beach adventure, I dressed two-year-old Kim in a rose-colored hand-knitted jacket. "Your jacket is so pretty," I said to her. "Grandma made it."

"Gamma made it," she repeated.

"That's right," I answered. "She made your favorite blanket and pajamas, too."

Minutes later we strolled hand-in-hand along a sandy path that led to the beach. Cool breezes wafted the sea's relentless roar through rustling grasses. We climbed a knoll, and suddenly blue-gray water rippled before us from horizon to horizon.

"Look, Kim!" I said. "The ocean! Who made it?"

Her innocent answer delighted me. "Gamma did!"

Because my mom lived nearly 1000 miles away and visits were rare, Kim's understanding about Grandma was largely based on things she saw—handmade clothing and gifts. Grandma was virtually invisible, but Kim believed she existed because the evidence proved it.

Kim's simple faith portrays a vital spiritual lesson. Tangible proofs encouraged her faith in an unseen Grandma's existence just as tangible proofs encourage our faith in our invisible God's existence.

Do you remember your unborn baby's first fluttering movements? Have you heard a woodpecker's insistent knocking or witnessed a hummingbird in flight? Admired a rainbow's pastel-tinted arch or gazed in wonder at snow-capped mountains shaded pink by a sunrise? Marveled at a giraffe's spots and a zebra's stripes and a monkey's hilarious chatter? Crunched through autumn's red and gold leaves or watched countless lacy snowflakes blanket the earth?

Creation confirms God's reality. But an even more convincing proof is found in His written Word. It predicted His Son's birth, life, death, and resurrection. Hundreds of years later, Jesus Christ fulfilled the prophecies. After His miraculous birth to a teenage virgin, He walked this earth for 33 years, died on a cross as a common criminal, and rose from the dead three days later. The New Testament records eyewitness accounts.

Transformed lives also evidence God's existence. When we commit ourselves to following Jesus Christ, He washes away sin's grime and gives us a fresh start. I've witnessed heroin addicts and alcoholics overcome substance abuse. I've seen broken marriages restored and former prostitutes regain dignity. Only a real, living God could perform such miracles in those who confess their sin and accept His forgiveness through Jesus Christ.

Some folks scoff at those who believe in and serve an invisible God. "Isn't that a little risky?" they ask. "Basing your whole life on someone you can't see?"

I would respond, "I can't see Him, but the evidence is in. And He loved me enough to send Jesus to pay my death penalty, so why should I be afraid?"

When circumstances seem chaotic, we can remember that the evidence is in. The invisible God is real, and He's in control. When life deals a harsh blow, we can look around and remember that God hasn't disappeared. The evidence overwhelmingly reassures us of His constant presence.

And with childlike faith, we can praise the invisible God!

Inward Glimpse

Heavenly Father, thank You for showing me Your greatness in countless ways. Help me to sense Your love every day as I see Your works and read Your Word.

- What evidence speaks to you of God's existence?
- Today's "One More Peek" mentions another evidence for God's existence. What is it?

Outward Glance

Father, thank You for revealing Yourself through Jesus. Draw _____ into a close relationship with You through Christ. As You do, make Your path of life known to him (Psalm 16:11). In righteousness may he see Your face. Satisfy him with seeing Your likeness (Psalm 17:15). Amen.

One More Peek

The wrath of God is being revealed from heaven against all the godlessness and wickedness of men who suppress the truth by their wickedness, since what may be known about God is plain to them, because God has made it plain to them. For since the creation of the world God's invisible qualities—his eternal power and divine nature—have been clearly seen, being understood from what has been made, so that men are without excuse (Romans 1:18-20).

The Script Writer

Trust in the LORD with all your heart
and lean not on your own understanding;
in all your ways acknowledge him,
and he will make your paths straight.
PROVERBS 3:5-6

Upward Gaze

Father, what is man that You care for him or think of him? (Psalm 144:3) You're worthy of praise because You are righteous in all Your ways and loving toward all You have made. You are near to all who call on You in truth. You fulfill the desires of those who fear You. You hear their cry and save them (Psalm 145:17-19). Amen.

***

Christmas Eve at the in-laws'. Tree lights sparkled, children danced and giggled, and true to tradition, adults gathered for a short prayer time.

Sandy curled close to her husband on the sofa. She glanced around the room as her relatives found seats. *It's a perfect scenario except for one thing,* she thought. *If I could write my life's script, I would add another little cousin, or perhaps two or three. Every year is the same—we're the only ones without children. Will the scene ever change?*

One by one, the in-laws praised and prayed. Sandy listened but scarcely caught their words. Instead, she heard the children's laughter. Their delighted squeals filled her thoughts with sweet sorrow. They accentuated her heart's emptiness—the void caused by infertility.

To Sandy's surprise, a sister-in-law crossed the room and wrapped her arms around her. Sensing Sandy's sadness, she spoke God-inspired words: "Weeping may remain for a night, but rejoicing comes in the morning" (Psalm 30:5).

The words soothed Sandy. As she pondered them, she realized that although they didn't promise her a baby, they guaranteed joy. She'd wept for several years already, but joy would eventually come. How and when, she didn't know.

Seven years passed. During that time, Sandy often wished she could rewrite her life's script. She wanted her role to include motherhood, not the empty arms of a woman labeled, "infertile for mysterious reasons."

Since childhood, she'd been accustomed to making things happen, but this was different. As much as she wanted to direct her own steps, God had other plans. He wanted her to relinquish control, remove herself from the director's chair, and let Him fully develop her character.

As Sandy yielded, she acknowledged that although she might never comprehend God's ways, she could trust His wisdom and rely on His daily strength. She discovered peace and joy amid disappointment.

One day, she discovered something else—she was pregnant! Before the next Christmas, she bore a son. Three years later, she delivered a daughter.

Through her ups and downs, Sandy embraced important truths— God writes our life's script, and He's a masterful Director. We don't always agree. Occasionally, when we flounder on the set, we feel as though He's enjoying an extended coffee break. We question His ways, His thoughts, His presence.

Some days we feel like grabbing the pen from His almighty hand and editing out the parts we don't like. But as we relinquish control, we find peace and joy in Him rather than in circumstances. We discover His wisdom, patience, love, faithfulness, and strength.

As we grow in our knowledge of God and obey His Word, our faith blossoms. Our negative or critical thought patterns change to thanksgiving and praise. We begin to see our life's script in light of eternity, from God's perspective.

Allowing God to direct our lives means trusting Him to accomplish His purposes even when we don't see or understand. It's applauding His directorship and giving Him a standing ovation when the curtain closes.

Inward Glimpse

Dear Father, thank You for writing my life's script with love. Help me trust You. Make my life what You want it to be. Amen.

- Write a prayer in which you thank God for not abandoning you to write your own script!
- Do you want to edit an aspect of your life? Ask the Lord to help you trust Him and give Him the opportunity to do what He pleases.

Outward Glance

Father, I pray that _____ will trust You to show him the way to go. May he lift up his soul to You. Teach him to do Your will, and by Your Spirit, lead him on level ground (Psalm 143:8,10). Amen.

One More Peek

Do not put your trust in princes,
in mortal men, who cannot save....
Blessed is he whose help is the God of Jacob,
whose hope is in the LORD his God,
the Maker of heaven and earth, the sea, and everything in
them—
the LORD, who remains faithful forever (Psalm 146:3,5-6).

Counterfeit Comfort

As a mother comforts her child,
so will I comfort you.
ISAIAH 66:13

Upward Gaze

Father, when I've said, "My foot is slipping," Your love has supported me. When anxiety has been great within me, Your consolation has brought joy to my soul (Psalm 94:18-19). Even though I walk through the valley of the shadow of death, I will fear no evil, for You are with me. Your rod and staff comfort me (Psalm 23:4). I'm comforted with the knowledge that Your promise renews my life (Psalm 119:50). Amen.

◄ MOM ►

When Kim was a toddler, one of her favorite comforts was a stuffed pink bear about five inches tall and one inch thick. She pushed her pointer finger through the satin ribbon loop on its head and held the plush animal close to her cheek while sucking her thumb. She packed that bear everywhere she went.

One evening after visiting friends in Seattle, we buckled the kids into their car seats, waved goodbye, and headed for home. The hour was late, and we were tired. And then it happened.

"Bear?" squeaked Kim.

"I'll find your bear," I promised. "It's probably in the diaper bag." I conducted a critter search, but to my despair, it was nowhere to be seen.

I offered a stuffed kitty instead, but Kim wasn't interested. A cracker couldn't distract her, either.

"Bear?" she peeped again. This time she sounded worried, even wounded. Her voice turned to a whimper and then a full-blown wail. I looked at Gene. He looked at me. He zipped off the freeway at the next exit and wound our van through the city to our friend's house. Within minutes, Kim's finger poked through the satin loop. She fell asleep with the fuzzy bear pressed against her cheek.

Her other favorite comfort was a crib-sized blanket her grandmother had sewn. She loved snuggling in its softness and dragging it behind her when she toddled through the house. Because I washed the well-traveled blankie often, it soon fell apart.

When I mentioned its tattered condition to my mom, she sprang into action. "I'll sew an identical blanket, but I'll use stronger backing this time," she said. "Kim will never know the difference."

Within a few days, the mailman delivered a package addressed to Kim. She ripped the brown wrapping and pulled out the new blanket. She stared at it for a moment and then looked at her old blanket. To our surprise, she threw the new one on the floor and stomped on it. "No!" she cried. "No blankie!"

We stifled our laughter. Kim scowled at the gift and retreated to a corner, hugging her old, frayed blanket. The tattered blankie was the one she loved; a counterfeit couldn't comfort her.

While security blankets, favorite toys, pacifiers, and thumbs comfort our children, we seek solace from other sources. Sometimes we turn to food, or we might dive into relationships, TV, work, or hobbies to escape distress. Counterfeits may bring temporary relief or distraction, but only God brings *lasting* comfort.

How does He do that? By reminding us of His precious promises: forgiveness for sin, peace in the midst of pain, joy instead of sorrow, strength to do what He has called us to do, and eternal life in heaven.

When we've received God's comfort, He wants us to pass it along to others rather than keep it to ourselves. Perhaps our spouse or children face difficult work or school situations and need a listening ear when they come home. Maybe a newly widowed or divorced mom needs a helping hand. Perhaps by exemplifying God's true comfort to hurting or anxious folks, we'll prevent them from seeking counterfeit comfort and help them find solace in the true Source.

Inward Glimpse

Dear Father, thank You for being the source of true comfort. When I'm in distress, remind me to turn to You rather than to a counterfeit. Amen.

- Have you sought counterfeit comfort? In what ways?
- Write a prayer, asking God to be your source of comfort and to help you share His comfort with others.

Outward Glance

Heavenly Father, when _____ feels sorrow or distress, please give him comfort and joy (Jeremiah 31:13). May he be comforted by Your ancient laws and unfailing love (Psalm 119:52,76). Thank You. Amen.

One More Peek

Praise be to the God and Father of our Lord Jesus Christ, the Father of compassion and the God of all comfort, who comforts us in all our troubles, so that we can comfort those in any trouble with the comfort we ourselves have received from God (2 Corinthians 1:3-4).

The Good Shepherd

The LORD is my shepherd,
I shall not be in want.
PSALM 23:1

Upward Gaze

Father, You are a loving shepherd. I praise You for tending Your flock, gathering Your lambs in Your arms and carrying them close to Your heart, and gently leading those with young (Isaiah 40:11). You're a marvelous shepherd. Thank You for rescuing the scattered and making them lie down in rich pastures (Ezekiel 34:11-15). Amen.

My only encounter with sheep happened when I was about five years old. I'd run down the hill behind Grandpa's farmhouse to see his livestock close-up. His solitary ram ambled toward me.

It wants me to pet it, I thought. *Nice sheep.* My perception changed when it broke into a run. Fearing for my life, I panicked and bolted uphill. The sound of approaching hooves pounded in my ears.

Suddenly I tripped and landed on the prairie grass with a thud. I lay paralyzed, too scared to move. *I'm dead! It's gonna eat me, and no one will ever know what happened!*

The creature stopped, sniffed, nudged me with its nose, licked my arm, and then sauntered away.

That's it? I thought. *All that panic for nothing?* I stood up, brushed the dirt from my clothes, and retreated to the farmhouse rather sheepishly (no pun intended!).

Even though I'm not an expert in sheep personalities, I would guess that ol' Fluff Ball was either curious, grouchy, or playing watchdog. Maybe I frightened the poor thing. In any case, it displayed baffling behavior.

Sheep are interesting animals. Rather than being smart and self-sufficient, they are perhaps one of the neediest genera God created. More than any other livestock, a flock of sheep requires limitless care from a knowledgeable and attentive shepherd. Surviving and thriving is impossible without his help.

A caring shepherd willingly invests time and energy into his animals because he values them. After purchasing them, he supplies them with a fresh water source and grazes them in green pastures—a feat sometimes requiring the clearing of rough, rocky terrain in order to grow succulent grasses. He provides needed veterinary care and keeps a watchful eye for predators.

If a sheep wanders from the flock, the shepherd searches until he finds it. Each minute counts, for if the sheep is "cast," having rolled onto its back, it will die quickly. The shepherd gently rolls it to its side and helps it stand. He rubs its limbs to restore circulation until the animal can walk again.

In his book *A Shepherd Looks at Psalm 23,* author Phillip Keller draws parallels between a shepherd caring for his flock and God caring for his people. He writes,

> It is no accident that God has chosen to call us sheep. The behavior of sheep and human beings is similar in many ways....Our mass mind (or mob instincts), our fears and timidity, our stubbornness and stupidity, our perverse habits are all parallels of profound importance.
>
> Yet, despite these adverse characteristics Christ chooses us, buys us, calls us by name, makes us His own and delights in caring for us.[2]

Keller is right. Just as a good shepherd purchases his sheep and calls them his own, so Christ has done the same. He paid the price, not with cash but with His own blood. He owns us, values us, and knows what will make us flourish.

As a shepherd works the land to produce the best food for his animals, so Christ works in our hearts through the Holy Spirit. He removes the rocks of bitterness and pride, sows the seeds of His Word, and produces crops of joy, peace, and contentment in our lives. He satisfies us with the best in exchange for the dry places where we find no fulfillment.

And as a shepherd shows compassion for his cast sheep, so Christ displays compassion towards men and women who are cast down—the discouraged, the frightened, or those for whom society has only unkind words. Rather than expressing disgust or annoyance with them, He reaches out to them in love, restores their souls, grants hope and joy, and removes shame and guilt.

Following Him as our Shepherd, we receive the very best care!

Inward Glimpse

Father, thank You for being my Shepherd. Help me trust Your loving care. Amen.

- According to today's "One More Peek," Jesus called Himself the "Good Shepherd." How has He fulfilled that role in your life?
- Read the hymn "Savior, like a Shepherd Lead Us" on page 69. Which stanza means the most to you, and why?

Outward Glance

Father, I pray that _____ will acknowledge You as her shepherd. Make her lie down in green pastures; lead her beside quiet waters. Restore her soul and guide her in paths of righteousness for Your name's sake. Comfort her with Your rod and staff when she walks through the valley of the shadow of death so that she might not fear any evil. Thank You, Good Shepherd (Psalm 23:2-4). Amen.

One More Peek

I am the good shepherd; I know my sheep and my sheep know me—just as the Father knows me and I know the Father—and I lay down my life for the sheep (John 10:14-15).

Savior, like a
Shepherd Lead Us

Dorothy A. Thrupp

Savior, like a shepherd lead us,
   Much we need Thy tender care;
In Thy pleasant pastures feed us,
   For our use Thy folds prepare;
Blessed Jesus, blessed Jesus,
   Thou hast bought us, Thine we are;
Blessed Jesus, blessed Jesus,
   Thou hast bought us, Thine we are.

We are Thine; do Thou befriend us,
   Be the Guardian of our way;
Keep Thy flock, from sin defend us,
   Seek us when we go astray;
Blessed Jesus, blessed Jesus,
   Hear, O hear us when we pray;
Blessed Jesus, blessed Jesus,
   Hear, O hear us when we pray.

Thou hast promised to receive us,
   Poor and sinful though we be;
Thou hast mercy to relieve us,
   Grace to cleanse and power to free;
Blessed Jesus, blessed Jesus,
   Early let us turn to Thee;
Blessed Jesus, blessed Jesus,
   Early let us turn to Thee.

The Stolen Earrings

If we confess our sins, he is faithful and just
and will forgive us our sins and
purify us from all unrighteousness.
1 JOHN 1:9

Upward Gaze

Heavenly Father, we see Your faithfulness every day in creation. You appoint the sun to shine by day and the moon and stars to shine by night. You stir up the sea so that its waves roar. The Lord Almighty is Your name. Thank You that in Your faithfulness You forgive our wickedness and remember our sins no more (Jeremiah 31:34). You will again have compassion on us; You will tread our sins underfoot and hurl all our iniquities into the depths of the sea (Micah 7:19). Amen.

MOM

Sitting in the back seat of our family's station wagon as it rolled down the highway toward Grandma and Grandpa's farm, I stared out the window and daydreamed about the weekend ahead. Aunts, uncles, cousins—they would all be there. *We're gonna have soooo much fun! We'll play with the kittens and chase the chickens....*

"Hey! Where did ya get these?" demanded my younger brother. I ignored him. After all, he *was* only my little brother.

"Hey!" he repeated. "Where did ya get these?" He punched me on the arm for emphasis.

I turned to him, ready to punch him back. But when I saw what his pudgy hand held, I froze. *Oh no! I'm dead!* As I'd daydreamed, he'd snooped through my purse and discovered a tiny pair of fake pearl earrings. Now he was holding up my dirty little secret for the whole world to see.

"I found them," I lied, lunging for the jewels. He hid them behind his back, beyond my reach.

"Look at what Grace had in her purse!" He thrust his fist past me and opened it under Mom's nose.

The interrogation began. The truth spilled out.

Several weeks earlier, while we were visiting relatives, a cousin had shown me her mom's jewelry. We'd tried on necklaces and earrings just for fun. The fake pearls captivated me, and when my cousin wasn't looking, I slipped them into my pocket. Naturally, I couldn't wear them in front of my parents, so I wore them only while playing at friends' homes. Despite my stealth, I'd been caught!

My aunt was sitting in Grandma's kitchen when we arrived at the farm. With knees knocking, I approached her and opened my hand to reveal the earrings.

"I took these from your jewelry box," I said, avoiding her eyes. Tears tumbled down my cheeks. "I'm sorry. Will you forgive me?"

"Of course I forgive you," she answered. "Thank you for returning them, Grace." Her hug and smile reassured me that everything was okay. For weeks I'd lived in fear of being caught, but instantly the guilt disappeared. I'd confessed, made restitution, received forgiveness, and felt free!

My aunt's forgiveness illustrates God's response to us when we confess our wrongdoings. He's quick to forgive because He wants our relationship restored. He doesn't want us haunted by guilt; He wants us to enjoy the freedom of a clear conscience.

That incident occurred 36 years ago. My aunt has never mentioned it. In fact, I'll bet she doesn't even remember it. That's also like God's response, for when we confess our sin and receive His gracious forgiveness, He never brings it up again.

What a great model for us! When our kids (or any other people, for that matter) seek our forgiveness, we have a wonderful opportunity to exemplify God's character. By forgiving and never bringing it up again, we model God's loving forgiveness, and other people see Him in us.

Inward Glimpse

Heavenly Father, thank You for unconditional forgiveness. Help me forgive other people the same way. I pray in Jesus' name. Amen.

- Describe the feeling of a clear conscience.
- Write a short prayer in which you thank God for His forgiveness.

Outward Glance

Thank You, God, for faithfully providing a way of escape when _____ is tempted to sin. Help her understand that no temptation has seized her except what is common to everybody, and You won't allow her to be tempted beyond what she can bear (1 Corinthians 10:13). Thank You for giving her a conscience. Please teach her the joy and freedom of a clear conscience. And just as You are faithful to forgive ____ _____ when she confesses her sin to You, teach her to forgive those who have sinned against her (Colossians 3:13). Amen.

One More Peek

I will heal my people and will let them enjoy abundant peace and security. I will bring Judah and Israel back from captivity and will rebuild them as they were before. I will cleanse them from all the sin they have committed against me and will forgive all their sins of rebellion against me. Then this city will bring me renown, joy, praise and honor before all nations (Jeremiah 33:6-9).

Spank Me!

Our fathers disciplined us for a little while
as they thought best;
but God disciplines us for our good,
that we may share in his holiness.
HEBREWS 12:10

Upward Gaze

Heavenly Father, I praise You for demonstrating tough love through Your discipline. It's not pleasant, but it teaches me how to live. You have a purpose: that I might share in Your holiness. I embrace Your ways, Father, for they will bring me righteousness and peace if I allow myself to be trained by them (Hebrews 12:6-11). Amen.

One afternoon, two-year-old Stephanie climbed onto the coffee table and posed like a puppy on four legs. "Honey, please climb down," I said. She stared at me innocently but didn't move.

I repeated the command in case she hadn't heard. "Please get off the coffee table." This time she shook her head. I prepared for battle. "Get off the coffee table *now.*" Defiantly, she patted herself on the bottom and said, "Spank me."

Not wanting to disappoint my daughter, I complied with her request. Did she enjoy the pain of discipline? I doubt it. Did she appreciate my efforts to teach through discipline? Nope. Did I enjoy administering the discipline? Not for a second.

Discipline isn't pleasant for either the giver or the recipient, but sometimes it's necessary, and the results are worth the pain and effort. In this instance, I know my actions proved effective because the scene never replayed itself. Why did they work? Possibly because Stephanie knew that I loved her, and in turn, she trusted me.

Sometimes my behavior resembles that of a two-year-old. In such instances, God administers discipline. Do I like it? About as much as Stephanie enjoyed her spanking.

For example, I met one of my friends recently at the local farmers' market. After the usual chitchat, I asked about her writing projects.

"I'm frustrated," she replied. "I can't find anyone who is able to help me move forward. I think I'll join an out-of-town writers' group."

Her words hurt my ego. Wasn't my help good enough? *Go ahead. Spend your money on gas,* I thought. My face flushed as I snapped, "You'll hear the same advice I've already given you." Instantly I knew I'd wronged her, but pride wouldn't let me recant. I said goodbye and stomped away like a pouting toddler.

Needless to say, that encounter haunted me. Each time I prayed, my friend's face entered my thoughts. Each time I read God's Word, my unkind words and haughty attitude hounded me. Each night when I closed my eyes to sleep, the conversation replayed itself in my mind.

"Make it right," the Holy Spirit prompted.

"I'm too busy writing my book about the character of God," I argued.

"Speak to her."

"Later. I'm praying now, and then I'll be busy writing an article about maintaining healthy relationships."

One morning I read from *My Utmost for His Highest* by Oswald Chambers: "As a child of God I am good only as I walk in the light....It is no use praying unless we are living as children of God."[3]

The quote grabbed my attention like a swat on the backside. The message was clear: I hadn't been living like a child of God, and my Father wanted me to change. I finally responded, accepting the correction as for my own good. I phoned my friend, apologized for my haughty attitude, and received her gracious forgiveness.

Just as we discipline our children to shape their character, God corrects us so that we might be conformed to the image of Jesus Christ. He does it from a loving heart and has only our good in mind. He wants to give us hope and a future (Jeremiah 29:11). Let's embrace His ways, knowing that He'll produce peace and righteousness in us.

Perhaps we can help our children understand spiritual discipline by telling them how God has worked in our lives. We should admit our own disobedience and tell how God disciplined us for our good. Knowing that Mom doesn't pretend to be perfect might be an encouragement to them!

Inward Glimpse

Dear Father, thank You for loving me enough to discipline me in righteousness. Help me remember that You want me to be holy as You are holy. I pray in Jesus' name. Amen.

- Write about a time when you experienced God's discipline. What did you learn?
- If you're struggling with God's discipline over an issue right now, ask Him to help you embrace His ways and learn from them. Write out that prayer.

Outward Glance

Dear Father, Your Word is full of instruction about discipline. I pray that _____ will heed correction and gain understanding (Proverbs 15:32). Keep her from ignoring discipline so she will not come to poverty and shame. Honor her as she heeds correction (Proverbs 13:18). May she receive discipline and show other people the way to life rather than ignoring it and leading them astray (Proverbs 10:17). When You discipline her, may she be blessed as You grant her relief from the days of trouble (Psalm 94:12-13). Amen.

One More Peek

The fear of the LORD is the beginning of knowledge,
but fools despise wisdom and discipline.
Listen, my son, to your father's instruction
and do not forsake your mother's teaching.
They will be a garland to grace your head
and a chain to adorn your neck (Proverbs 1:7-9).

A Perfect Balance

What shall we say, then?
Shall we go on sinning so that grace may increase?
By no means! We died to sin; how can we live in it any longer?
ROMANS 6:1-2

Upward Gaze

Heavenly Father, You are kind and forgiving, abounding in love to all who call to You (Psalm 86:5). You are also holy. There is no one holy like You, no Rock like You (1 Samuel 2:2). In You, love and faithfulness meet together; righteousness and peace kiss each other (Psalm 85:10). Amen.

My friend Jan treasures her sons' bedtimes because the boys frequently ask thought-provoking questions. When she talks with them, Jan gains understanding into their spiritual development. She often leaves their rooms challenged in her own faith.

On one occasion, five-year-old Matthew gave her a fresh glimpse into the perfect balance between God's holiness and His mercy, and how they apply to a believer's life.

That evening, Jan had decided to teach him the ACTS prayer model (adoration, confession, thanksgiving, supplication). *I'll do it slowly,* she thought. *I'll begin by telling him about confession.*

She launched into her lesson. "Sometimes we do things God doesn't want us to do," she explained. "Confession means we tell God what we've done. When we do that, He forgives us—He wipes our slate clean. We start over again."

To illustrate her point, she led Matthew through a confession prayer. The instant Jan whispered "Amen," she heard her son's voice. "Mom?"

"Yes, Sweetie?"

"If I confess at bedtime, can I do whatever I want all day long?"

Jan didn't know whether to laugh or cry!

Matthew's logic mimics that of many adults. "Do what I want? Sure, why not? I'm safe because God promises to forgive my sins if I confess them." They assume God's forgiveness grants them liberty to live as they please today, confess tonight, and wake up with a clean slate tomorrow. They're overlooking the fact that although God forgives sin because He is merciful, He also punishes sin because He is holy.

The apostle Paul addresses this issue in his letter to the Romans. He responds to their rationalization with a simple answer: "By no means! We died to sin; how can we live in it any longer?" In other words, if we've received Jesus Christ as our personal Savior, our lives should reflect His holy character. We should be running away from sin rather than dabbling in it. We're no longer slaves to sin but slaves to God—a relationship that leads to holy living (Romans 6:22).

Because we're mere mortals, however, we succumb to temptation and sin. In God's mercy, He forgives us and restores us to fellowship with Him once more, all because of Jesus' death on Calvary.

His perfect balance between holiness and mercy sets an example for my parenting practices. When I'm upset or tired, I'm sometimes tempted to deal too harshly with my kids, delivering discipline far beyond what their crimes deserve. The scale tips heavily to one side. At those times, God reminds me of the mercy He's shown toward me.

On other occasions, I'm tempted to let sin slide because, after all, "it's not a big deal." The scale tips too far to the other side. With a quiet nudge, God reminds me of His holiness and His desire for us to be like Him.

The perfect balance. God—the perfect model.

Inward Glimpse

Dear Father, in You lies the perfect balance of mercy and holiness. Help me to walk in holiness as You do, but also to remember that Your mercy is there for me when I fail. Help me model that to my children. Thank You. Amen.

- Do you tend to tip the scales more heavily toward mercy or holiness?
- Write a prayer in which you ask God to give you a deeper understanding of His perfect balance, and to help you experience that balance in your life.

Outward Glance

Father, please help _____ lead a blameless life. Help her trust You without wavering. Test her and try her. Examine her heart and mind. Keep Your love ever before her, and help her walk continually in Your truth (Psalm 26:2-3). Amen.

One More Peek

I do not hide your righteousness in my heart;
  I speak of your faithfulness and salvation.
I do not conceal your love and your truth
  from the great assembly.
Do not withhold your mercy from me, O LORD;
  may your love and your truth always protect me
  (Psalm 40:10-11).

Always the Same

Every good and perfect gift is from above,
coming down from the Father of the heavenly lights,
who does not change like shifting shadows.
JAMES 1:17

Upward Gaze

Heavenly Father, You're worthy of praise because You never change (Malachi 3:6). You are robed in majesty and armed with strength. You have firmly established the world so it cannot be moved. Your throne was established long ago; You are from all eternity (Psalm 93:1-2). For ever and ever You are the same. Amen.

MOM

"Mom, I'm hungry!" called six-year-old Christopher from the basement, where he and his younger brother entertained themselves with building blocks and toy cars. "Can I have a snack?"

Lynay looked at the clock. Dinner would be ready in less than an hour. "Not now," she replied. "We'll eat soon. I don't want you to ruin your appetite."

"Aw, Mom," he whined.

"You heard me."

The doorbell rang before Christopher could argue. Lynay opened the door to find a shivering tenth-grader standing on the step. Lynay recognized her as a member of her husband's youth group. "Hi! What's up?" The teen's distressed expression said it all.

Oh-oh. Looks like a counseling session, Lynay thought. *I hope the boys will stay occupied for a while longer.* She invited the high-schooler into the living room, motioned for her to sit on the couch, and sat beside her.

"So, how's it going?" asked Lynay.

"Not good," the girl said. "I need your advice."

As Lynay listened to the teen's complicated tale, she heard a cupboard door open and close. Excusing herself, she peeked around the corner and saw Christopher standing in the center of the kitchen.

"What are you doing?" she asked.

"Nothing."

Lynay wasn't convinced, but she couldn't press the issue. The girl needed her attention. "I'll talk to you later," she said as she turned away.

After the teen left, Lynay looked at the clock. Her husband would be home soon. The kids were hungry. She'd rather prepare a salad and set the table, but she remembered her promise to her son—"I'll talk to you later."

Lynay joined Christopher downstairs. To her disappointment, she found several candy wrappers lying on the floor beside him. "What's this?" she asked, pointing at the pile.

"I ate candy," he admitted.

"I said you couldn't have a snack before dinner. Didn't you believe me?"

"I thought you were too busy to notice," he replied honestly.

Dinner was delayed, but that didn't matter. Mother and son had a good talk about obedience and honesty. Lynay's experience reinforced her desire to be consistent with her children.

She sets a good example. Sometimes ignoring our kids' actions is easier than confronting them, especially when we're tired, stressed, or distracted. If a child or teen tests the behavior boundaries repeatedly in a short period of time, we're tempted to disregard the offense to avoid dealing with yet another negative issue.

When we practice consistency, however, our children learn that we mean what we say. They learn that disobedience carries consequences, just as good behavior warrants rewards.

This principle applies to our spiritual life because, like a perfect father, God is consistent with His children. Scripture teaches His boundaries and warns of consequences for stepping over them. He never ignores sin. Disregarded warnings produce negative results. We reap what we sow.

Likewise, God fulfills His promises to reward righteous living. Sometimes we don't see those rewards realized in our lifetime. But heaven's coming, and the rewards for our obedience far exceed our wildest imagination!

God's consistency with us reflects His unchanging, ever-reliable character. He remains the same forever, unaltered by moods or circumstances or age, and that consistency provides security for us, just as our consistency provides security for our kids.

Inward Glimpse

Dear Father, thank You for being consistent. Help me reflect that quality to my children so they can understand You more fully. Amen.

- Do you struggle with inconsistency in any area of your life? If so, what is it?
- Hebrews 13:8 says that Jesus is the same yesterday, today, and forever. How does that encourage you today?

Outward Glance

Father, I pray that _____ will recognize Your Word as eternally true. May she understand that your faithfulness continues throughout all generations and Your laws endure to this day (Psalm 119: 89-91). Help her consistently follow You and reflect Your character to other people around her. Amen.

One More Peek

In the beginning you laid the foundations of the earth,
    and the heavens are the work of your hands.
They will perish, but you remain;
    they will all wear out like a garment.
Like clothing you will change them
    and they will be discarded.
But you remain the same,
    and your years will never end (Psalm 102:25-27).

The Beauty of Holiness

One thing I ask of the LORD,
this is what I seek:
that I may dwell in the house of the LORD
all the days of my life,
to gaze upon the beauty of the LORD
and to seek him in his temple.
PSALM 27:4

Upward Gaze

There is no one holy like You, Lord (1 Samuel 2:2). How can I stand before You? No shred of sin or impurity resides in Your character. No god is as great as You (Psalm 77:13). You reign, great and exalted over all the nations—let the nations tremble! Let them praise Your great and awesome name, for You alone are holy (Psalm 99:1-3). Amen.

◄ MOM ►

"Your skin is like velvet," someone told me a long, long time ago. The comment pampered my pride, but not for long. A few months later, puberty pasted a pimple squarely on my chin, another on my forehead, and a third somewhere in between. Velvety skin disintegrated into something resembling burlap.

I spent hard-earned baby-sitting money on every product that promised new, fresh radiance. I tried everything—astringents, miracle creams, mud masks, oatmeal paste, cucumber slices.

Did my skin clear up? Oh, to be so lucky! Instead, I discovered an allergy to a leading face cream. Cold sores erupted on my lips at the mere thought of it!

Time eventually cleared my skin, but it hasn't changed society's definition of beauty. We all know what it is—a Barbie-doll figure, long sleek hair, flawless skin, and a gorgeous smile. Each year women spend gazillions of dollars on cosmetics, makeovers, miracle diets, and exercise equipment to satisfy society's standard.

The funny thing is, outward beauty is relative. What other cultures consider beautiful, we might consider outrageous. How would you like to sport a giraffe-like neck as the women of the Karen Padaung tribe do, or a tattooed face like the women of the Kondh tribe?

History set its own standards, too. Incredibly tiny waistlines and massive white wigs hanging heavy with ringlets were once the rage. If beauty standards change over time and according to culture, what constitutes true beauty in a woman's life?

A holy life.

In her book, *Behold Your God*, Myrna Alexander says,

> The beauty of holiness is the natural majestic beauty brilliantly present when evil is absent. Consider, for an earthly example, a sparkling mountain stream fed by melting snow. This picture stands in sharp contrast to the ugliness of a stagnant, murky pond filled with smelly waste and soiled food wrappers.[4]

Consider the beauty of God's holiness as seen in Jesus Christ. Scripture says that although He was tempted in every way as we are, He didn't sin. His life was pure, like a crystal-clear mountain stream, free from the filth of selfishness, impure thoughts, and jealousy. He treated others with respect, meeting their needs and displaying a servant's heart by washing their feet. His unconditional love held Him on the cross, making salvation possible for all who believe in His name.

We get to know Jesus more intimately by spending time reading God's Word and praying. And as we walk in obedience, our lives reflect true beauty—the beauty of holiness. When we wipe up spilled apple juice, drive our kids to yet another baseball game without complaining, welcome new neighbors with a plate of freshly baked cookies, or cook a meal for a shut-in, others will recognize the beauty of Jesus in our lives and be drawn to it.

When the world's concept of beauty leaves us struggling with feelings of inferiority, we can ask God to set us free. He loves us passionately and longs to see us become women of true beauty who touch the lives of those around us with His love.

Inward Glimpse

Dear Father, thank You for Jesus' example of a holy life. Develop that holiness in me so the beauty of His character will shine in a hurting world and draw others to You. I pray in Jesus' name. Amen.

- Allow the Holy Spirit to show you areas of your life that need to change. What are they? Write them down and ask God to develop His holiness in every aspect of your life.

- Meditate on the words of the song "Take Time to Be Holy," printed on page 88. Which stanza means the most to you, and why?

Outward Glance

Holy Father, I pray that _____'s walk will be blameless. Help him daily choose what is right and speak the truth from his heart (Psalm 15:1-2). May he have clean hands and a pure heart. May he never lift up his soul to an idol or swear by a false god (Psalm 24:3-5). Strengthen his heart so he will be blameless and holy in Your presence when Jesus returns someday (1 Thessalonians 3:13). Amen.

One More Peek

I dressed you in fine linen and covered you with costly garments....You became very beautiful and rose to be a queen. And your fame spread among the nations on account of your beauty, because the splendor I had given you made your beauty perfect, declares the Sovereign LORD (Ezekiel 16:10,13-14).

Take Time
to Be Holy

William Longstaff

Take time to be holy, speak oft with thy Lord;
Abide in Him always, and feed on His Word.
Make friends of God's children; help those who are weak;
Forgetting in nothing His blessing to seek.

Take time to be holy, the world rushes on;
Much time spend in secret with Jesus alone;
By looking to Jesus, like Him thou shalt be;
Thy friends in thy conduct His likeness shall see.

Take time to be holy, be calm in thy soul;
Each thought and each motive beneath His control;
Thus led by His Spirit to fountains of love,
Thou soon shalt be fitted for service above.

True Love

And now these three remain:
faith, hope and love.
But the greatest of these is love.
1 CORINTHIANS 13:13

Upward Gaze

Father, Your love reaches to the heavens, Your faithfulness to the skies. Your unfailing love is priceless (Psalm 36:5,7). My lips glorify You, for Your love is better than life itself (Psalm 63:3). I will declare that it stands firm forever (Psalm 89:1). Amen.

◄ MOM ►

Sixteen-year-old Josh propped his skateboard against the garage wall and entered the house. "Hi, Mom. I'm home!" he called.

"Hi! Glad you're back," his mother, Angie, answered from the kitchen. "Did you have a good time at the skateboard park?"

"Yeah, it was great. Only two major wipeouts." He grinned sheepishly and pointed at his jeans' ripped-out right knee.

"Jeans can be mended," Angie said, handing her son a peanut butter and jelly sandwich.

"Thanks, Mom," said Josh. He devoured the snack and headed out the door again.

Angie watched him leave. *He's changed so much,* she thought. *It's hard to believe he's the same boy who broke my heart the past two years.*

She poured a cup of herbal tea, settled into an overstuffed chair, and opened her journal. The handwritten entries exposed her past pain.

Josh lied to us today, she'd penned. *He attended an inappropriate movie and tried to hide it from his dad and me. He doesn't care about doing what's right—he's interested only in following his feelings. Where will his attitude lead?*

Angie flipped to another entry posted one week later. *I smelled smoke in the garage when I arrived home after shopping this afternoon. Josh and his friends later confessed to playing with open flames and pressurized spray cans. God, give me wisdom. What am I to do?*

Other accounts detailed Josh's rebellion—drinking alcohol, making small homemade bombs, flaunting an "I'll do what I want" attitude. They divulged a mother's frustration when her counsel fell on his deaf ears. They disclosed sleepless nights when she worried about her son's increasingly willful disobedience. They revealed her earnest prayers and her temptation to give up on Josh.

They also recorded God's gentle response. *Don't give up. Love Josh the way I love you. That's all I want you to do.*

Angie recalled flipping to the Bible's well-known passage describing true love: "Love is patient, love is kind…it is not easily angered, it keeps no record of wrongs. Love does not delight in evil but rejoices with the truth. It always protects, always trusts, always hopes, always perseveres" (1 Corinthians 13:4-7).

She had thought that true love's characteristics surpassed her capabilities. How could she remain patient with her belligerent son? How could she refrain from anger at his back talk? How could she *not* keep a mental record of his stupid stunts?

Over and over, God faithfully prodded her to love Josh unconditionally, just as He loved her. It hadn't been easy, but Angie obeyed. She treated Josh respectfully but held him accountable for his wrongdoings. Chores well-done, homework completed on schedule, and other glimmers of positive progress brought sincere praise. Private and corporate prayer with close friends upheld her as she applied 1 Corinthians 13.

The battle was worth the effort.

God answered her prayers through a Christian teacher's spoken words. She wasn't even sure what he'd said, but Josh had responded, and that's all that mattered. Now he expressed concern for fellow students making poor choices. He checked Internet resources regarding movie recommendations. He respected curfews and kept his parents informed as to his whereabouts.

Once again, Angie recorded her thoughts. This time victory resounded. *God's unconditional love never fails.*

Indeed, God's unconditional love changes lives. Angie witnessed it through Josh's turnaround. If we've faced similar situations with our own children, we can relate to her thankful heart.

If our prayers haven't been answered yet and we're wondering how long our children will take to come to their senses, we can be encouraged—God loves our sons and daughters unconditionally. We must persevere in prayer and practice loving them as the Lord does.

Inward Glimpse

Dear Father, thank You for loving me unconditionally. Help me communicate that love to my children. Amen.

- Describe the father's love for his wayward son in Luke 15:11-24.

- Write a prayer in which you thank God for His unconditional love for you.

Outward Gaze

Father, please teach _____ to trust in Your unfailing love. May his heart rejoice in Your salvation (Psalm 13:5). Keep Your love always before him; teach him to walk consistently in Your truth (Psalm 26:3). When he faces difficult times, make Your face shine on him, and save him in Your unfailing love (Psalm 31:16). Amen.

One More Peek

But while he was still a long way off, his father saw him and was filled with compassion for him; he ran to his son, threw his arms around him and kissed him....The father said to his servants, "Quick! Bring the best robe and put it on him. Put a ring on his finger and sandals on his feet. Bring the fattened calf and kill it. Let's have a feast and celebrate. For this son of mine was dead and is alive again; he was lost and is found" (Luke 15:20,22-24).

Look on the Heart

*But the LORD said to Samuel, "Do not consider his appearance
or his height, for I have rejected him. The LORD does not
look at the things man looks at. Man looks at the
outward appearance, but the LORD looks at the heart."*
1 SAMUEL 16:7

Upward Gaze

Father, You're worthy of praise because no one is holy
like You, nor is any Rock like You. We will silence our boast-
ing and arrogance because You know everything and weigh
our actions. You break the bows of the mighty, but You
strengthen those who stumble (1 Samuel 2:2-4). Amen.

Mark's premature birth and cerebral palsy opened a new world for
Lorraine. Working with medical and educational professionals, she
helped set Mark's developmental goals. Mom and son frequented
doctors' offices and hospital outpatient clinics. They attended physical therapy sessions and early intervention classes.

When Mark was a toddler, Lorraine valued time spent with other
mothers of special-needs children. Every Tuesday morning, a half-dozen
moms swapped ideas, shared their past week's parenting ups and downs,
and received instruction from occupational and speech therapists.

Lorraine looked forward to the weekly sessions. She felt safe,
surrounded by others who understood her joys and frustrations. In this

room, no one stared at Mark. No one asked, "What's wrong with that boy? Why does he walk funny?"

The folks in this room were different from the general public. While they acknowledged her son's physical handicap, they looked beyond it to embrace the little boy's heart. They saw Mark, the boy who loved finger painting and chocolate pudding. They recognized his potential and planned activities to help develop it. Each 90-minute session recharged Lorraine's emotional batteries.

Lorraine faced a rude awakening when Mark started school. Her easygoing child developed stomachaches. Morning after morning, he cried, "I don't want to go to school."

She questioned Mark and expressed her concern to his teacher. She volunteered at the school and observed the goings-on. Before long she discovered the source of his unhappiness. Each time he approached other kids, either in the classroom or on the playground, they ran away, mocking—"You walk funny" or "You're weird" or "We don't want you here."

Lorraine's heart broke. *They're judging him by his outward appearance,* she thought. *They're not giving him a chance because they don't understand what he's like on the inside. I'll fix that.*

She asked his teacher for an opportunity to speak with the class about cerebral palsy. She hosted a Saturday afternoon party for Mark's classmates and encouraged her son to invite peers home after school and on weekends. She prayed that the children would look on her son's heart rather than his exterior appearance.

Her efforts paid off. Over time, the children understood that in spite of his physical challenges, Mark sparkled with spunk and enthusiasm. They discovered that he enjoyed the same computer games and videos they did. They looked past his crutches and saw his heart—the same heart God had seen and loved all along.

God is so good, isn't He? Like Lorraine, her friends, and eventually the school children, He looks beyond our physical abilities or disabilities. He accepts us regardless of our skin color or ethnic background. He treasures us even if we struggle with our weight or have bad hair days. He values us whether we're outgoing or shy, career-minded professionals or stay-at-home moms. Nothing about our outward person or accomplishments lessens or increases His love for us.

May that truth encourage us today! And may it encourage others as we model it. Let's treat others with respect and kindness in every circumstance. We'll exemplify God's mind and heart for mankind by refusing to buckle under society's pressure to gauge a person's worth according to his outward appearance.

Inward Glimpse

Dear Father, thank You for seeing my heart and not just my outward appearance. Help me reflect that attitude to others so they will understand more about Your love. Amen.

- Do you place more value on people who are outwardly attractive or publicly successful than those who are less appealing or who work behind the scenes? If so, write a prayer in which you ask God for forgiveness. Ask the Lord to change your heart so you will see people as He does.

- Look for an opportunity to speak with your children about this important truth. Perhaps you could encourage them to list positive character qualities about peers or other people they know whose outward appearance doesn't reach society's "acceptable" status.

Outward Glance

Father, I pray that _____ will serve You with a whole heart and a willing mind. May she understand that You search all hearts and understand the motive behind every thought (1 Chronicles 28:9). Help her understand Your value system—that what men value highly is often detestable in Your sight (Luke 16:15), and that You place more worth on a person's heart condition than on his or her outward appearance (1 Samuel 16:7). Amen.

One More Peek

Search me, O God, and know my heart;
test me and know my anxious thoughts.
See if there is any offensive way in me,
and lead me in the way everlasting (Psalm 139:23-24).

Ernie

I praise you because I am fearfully and wonderfully made;
your works are wonderful,
I know that full well.
PSALM 139:14

Upward Gaze

Father, You are the Lord, who has made all things. You alone stretched out the heavens and spread the earth (Isaiah 44:24). You've performed many wonders. The things You planned for us, no one can recount. They are too numerous to count (Psalm 40:5). Amen.

"This year's Christmas concert setting is a toy store," explained our pastor's wife to a group of restless Sunday school kids. "I want everyone to dress like a toy or a storybook character."

"I want to be a ballerina doll," said a little girl with long, blond curls.

"I'll be a robot," perked the boy beside her.

"I'll be Ernie," chimed Stephanie. She was four years old and an avid fan of "Sesame Street" buddies Ernie and Bert.

Ernie? I wondered. *How can we convert beautiful, blond, fair-skinned Stephanie into black-haired, red-nosed, orange-faced Ernie?*

Finding a shirt was easy. Someone had given her a red, yellow, and blue striped shirt that matched Ernie's. A nose? I found a red sponge clown nose at a costume shop. With a few snips here and there, it fit her face. A special glue dab held it in place. The hair? A carefully stitched piece of black furry material from a fabric store did the job. And the orange skin? Face paint.

Stephanie could have passed as Ernie's twin. Even Bert wouldn't have known the difference!

Kids filed on stage, each taking their place in the toy store. Stephanie stood in the front row, wedged between Raggedy Ann and a miniature tin soldier. All eyes fixed on her—the orange face and bulbous red nose drew attention like sugar water draws a hummingbird. Her stellar performance disappointed no one!

Later, a friend commented on Stephanie's choice to mimic Ernie. "I think it's great," my friend said, laughing. "Some kids would feel too self-conscious dressed like that, but Stephanie doesn't care. She's comfortable being herself!"

My friend's statement stayed with me for a long time. I rejoiced in its truth and prayed that my daughter's ability to accept herself would grow with her into adolescence and adulthood.

For us womenfolk, being comfortable with ourselves physically sometimes presents a challenge. If you're anything like me, you find yourself looking in the mirror and wondering what happened! *Where did my size-eight waistline go? Where did those stray gray hairs come from? What's with those tiny wrinkles around my eyes?* Sigh.

If we brood too long, we will begin comparing ourselves with other women. *If only my hair looked like hers. If only my complexion would glow like hers does. If only my wardrobe didn't scream, "Thrift store!" If only, if only, if only.* Before long we feel like the perfect candidate for a magazine makeover. We worry that we have nothing to offer anyone.

The only way to beat the broods is to remember that God loves us just the way we are. Our worth isn't based on our dress size or physical appearance. It's based solely on the fact that God loves us unconditionally. His love for us doesn't change if our dress size increases. He doesn't love us less than the gorgeous neighbor down the street. He simply loves us with a never-ending, wide-as-the-universe love.

Inward Glimpse

Father God, thank You for loving me the way I am. Help me rest in that knowledge and not worry about earning Your love. Amen.

- Do you have difficulty accepting an aspect of yourself? If so, what is it?
- How does God's Word say you are formed (Genesis 1:26-27; Psalm 139:13-16)?

Outward Glance

Dear Father, Your hands formed _____. Please give her understanding to learn Your commands (Psalm 119:73). Help her understand that You shaped and molded her (Job 10:8). Teach her knowledge and good judgment (Psalm 119:66) and make her heart blameless toward Your decrees so she may not be put to shame (Psalm 119:80). Amen.

One More Peek

Know that the LORD is God.
It is he who made us, and we are his;
we are his people, the sheep of his pasture (Psalm 100:3).

Walking by the Rules

I guide you in the way of wisdom
and lead you along straight paths.
When you walk, your steps will not be hampered;
when you run, you will not stumble.
PROVERBS 4:11-12

Upward Gaze

Dear God, I praise You for being a loving Father to me. Because You are truth, I follow Your example and walk in truth (Psalm 25:5). Because You are light and Your Word is a lamp, I'll walk and not stumble or be afraid (Psalm 119:105). Even though I walk through the valley of the shadow of death, I won't fear evil because You are my companion (Psalm 23:4). I praise You, for You are good and upright, instructing sinners in Your ways and guiding the humble in what is right (Psalm 25:8-9). Amen.

MOM

"Come here, Kim," I coaxed. "Come to Mommy!" I knelt on the floor and extended my arms toward my 14-month-old daughter. Her pudgy legs tottered as she stepped forward.

"She's doing it!" cheered her brother, Matthew. "Do it again, Kimmy."

Kim giggled with pride at her accomplishment and then cautiously placed one foot in front of the other again. Before long she'd toddled across the living room to my waiting arms and then returned to Matthew. Kim's success instantly turned into a game; she teetered back and forth across the room amid her audience's delighted squeals and cheers.

Kim's newly discovered independence launched me into months of careful supervision and training. Because we lived on a busy street without sidewalks, traffic posed a threat whenever we went for a walk. "I want you to hold my hand," I instructed. "We must be careful when we're on the road."

Kim obeyed until an abandoned toy or a neighbor's sleeping dog distracted her. Then she tried to wrestle her hand from mine so she could dart across the street. She fussed and whined when I refused to let her go. Her limited understanding told her that the hand-holding rule hindered her freedom.

As a parent, however, I knew better. The rule wasn't designed to make my daughter miserable; its purpose was to ensure her safety. Because I loved her, I wanted her to enjoy a long and safe life.

Like a loving parent, God has given us rules for life. Because He knows us intimately and understands what's best for us, He has designed them for our good. I hate to admit it, but at times I've behaved like my toddler. I've strained to free myself from God's grip because I didn't appreciate His rules. Consider, for instance, His command to give thanks in everything.

A couple of years ago, Stephanie applied for a position as a counselor-in-training at the camp where we work. Although we knew positions were limited, we felt confident that as a staff kid, she would receive an acceptance letter. Things didn't turn out the way we'd hoped.

Stephanie's face fell when she opened her letter and read that the positions had been filled. I watched her response and wanted to protect her from the hurt. Expressing gratitude was the last thing I felt like doing, but I knew the rule: "Give thanks in all circumstances, for this is God's will for you in Christ Jesus" (1 Thessalonians 5:18).

I faced a choice—be grateful that God's sovereignty was directing Stephanie's path, or run headlong into territory potholed with anger. Making a deliberate choice, I began thanking God that He was in control of circumstances. Doing so removed my negative emotions. It lifted my spirits and put my focus back on the Lord rather than on my disappointment. Stephanie learned the importance of giving thanks in everything. And by the way, she applied at a different camp, was accepted, and enjoyed a summer experience richer than she could have imagined!

God's rules, such as praying without ceasing, being joyful in all circumstances, respecting others, and being anxious for nothing, show His love for us. We might not always understand His guidelines or feel like obeying, but they're for our benefit. Should we pull our hand from His and realize our folly later, we can know He always welcomes us back.

Our willingness to walk according to God's rules affects those around us. Our children watch and often imitate us. Our obedience teaches them the importance of embracing God's rules for their own lives.

Inward Glimpse

Heavenly Father, thank You for guiding me. Help me trust You as we walk through life together, hand in hand. I pray in Jesus' name. Amen.

- Name two rules God has given in His Word. How does He show His love through them?
- Write a prayer of thanks to the Lord for walking with you and guarding your path.

Outward Glance

Father, I pray that _____ will recognize Your ways as loving and faithful (Psalm 25:10). May she trust You with all her heart and not lean on her own understanding. Make her paths straight as she acknowledges You in all her ways (Proverbs 3:5-6). Help her to consider Your ways and turn her steps to Your commandments (Psalm 119:59). Amen.

One More Peek

[I will] gather them from the ends of the earth....I will lead them beside streams of water on a level path where they will not stumble, because I am Israel's father, and Ephraim is my firstborn son (Jeremiah 31:8-9).

Unconditional Forgiveness

But God demonstrates his own love for us in this:
While we were still sinners, Christ died for us.
ROMANS 5:8

Upward Gaze

Father, I enter Your gates with thanksgiving and Your courts with praise. I give thanks to You, for You've blessed me with Your unconditional love and acceptance. You've given Jesus Christ to pay the price of my forgiveness. Blessed be Your name, for You are good! Your love endures forever, and Your faithfulness continues through all generations (Psalm 100:4-5). Amen.

MOM

Children are great teachers, especially on the topic of forgiveness. My kids are professionals in that field—I've given them plenty of practice!

One evening I knelt beside Stephanie's bed. She looked at me, her eyes betraying the hurt my impatience had caused before bedtime. "I'm sorry for yelling at you," I confessed. "I was wrong. Would you please forgive me?"

Without hesitation she threw her arms around my neck. "I love you, Mommy," she said. "Of course I forgive you."

Stephanie's sweet spirit humbled me. I returned the hug. "Thank you, Steph. I love you, too." As I tucked her in and left the room, I marveled at her easy, immediate response to my request.

She bore no grudges. She issued no warnings—"You'd better not do it again or else...." She declared no conditions—"I'll forgive you if you let me stay up another hour." My daughter simply said, "Of course I forgive you," and sealed her declaration with a hug.

Stephanie's gracious spirit reflects our heavenly Father's loving heart toward us when we confess our sin to Him. Scripture says that when we confess our sin, He's faithful to forgive us. He doesn't issue warnings—"I'll forgive you now, but it's the last time. Do you understand?" He doesn't forgive with conditions—"I'll forgive you if you memorize the book of Genesis." God forgives because Jesus Christ died for us.

Sometimes we're called to forgive even if the offender never asks for forgiveness. God's love living in us makes that possible. Several years ago I met a mother who demonstrated this in an amazing way.

One week after the Colombine High School shootings in Littleton, Colorado, Diane Lang's 17-year-old son was shot and killed while walking down his school hallway in a quiet Alberta town. No one would have blamed her for feeling angry toward the 14-year-old boy who pulled the trigger, but Diane chose to forgive.

The entire nation watched her and her husband model God's unconditional forgiveness. As a result, the Langs have presented the gospel repeatedly in schools across Canada, and their town's churches recently opened an interdenominational drop-in center for youth.

Diane's loving, kind response was a miracle of sorts, a miracle of God's love pouring through a human being incapable of doing such a thing in her own strength. What a fantastic example of God's love and forgiveness!

How do we respond when others disappoint or offend us? Do we respond with impatience? A grudge? The silent treatment? Or do we display God's forgiveness?

Like Diane, we can allow Christlike attitudes to rule our response to offenses. When our children disobey, we can model unconditional forgiveness. If our spouse or a coworker or family member hurts us, we can forgive because the Holy Spirit lives within us and enables us to do what is right.

When I'm faced with the need to forgive an offender, I'm reminded that I'm not perfect either *(ouch!)*, and in my lifetime I'll give others plenty of opportunities to extend forgiveness to me, too.

Inward Glimpse

Heavenly Father, thank You for offering unconditional forgiveness to me. Help me do the same for others. Amen.

- Meditate on the hymn "And Can It Be That I Should Gain?" printed on page 108. Write a couple of sentences explaining what God's unconditional love and forgiveness mean to you.

- How can you show your love in a special way to each member of your family this week? Write out your plan. Record their responses.

Outward Glance

Heavenly Father, I pray that Christ may dwell in _____ __'s heart through faith. I pray that he, being rooted and established in love, may have power, together with all the saints, to grasp how wide and long and high and deep Your love is. May he know this love that surpasses knowledge and be filled to the measure of all the fullness of God. Thank you for loving _____ with a love that knows no limit (Ephesians 3:17-19). When he sins, may he understand that Your forgiveness flows from this boundless love, and may he be quick to forgive others the same way. Amen.

One More Peek

The older brother became angry and refused to go in. So his father went out and pleaded with him...."My son" the father said, "you are always with me, and everything I have is yours. But we had to celebrate and be glad, because this brother of yours was dead and is alive again; he was lost and is found" (Luke 15:28,31-32).

And Can It Be
That I Should Gain?

Charles Wesley

And can it be that I should gain
   An interest in the Savior's blood?
Died He for me, who caused His pain?
   For me, who Him to death pursued?
Amazing love! how can it be
   That Thou, my God, shouldst die for me?

He left His Father's throne above,
   So free, so infinite His grace;
Emptied Himself of all but love,
   And bled for Adam's helpless race;
'Tis mercy all, immense and free;
   For, O my God, it found out me.

Long my imprisoned spirit lay,
   Fastbound in sin and nature's night;
Thine eye diffused a quick'ning ray,
   I woke, the dungeon flamed with light;
My chains fell off, my heart was free;
   I rose, went forth, and followed Thee.

No condemnation now I dread;
   Jesus, and all in Him, is mine!
Alive in Him, my living Head,
   And clothed in righteousness Divine,
Bold I approach th'eternal throne,
   And claim the crown, through Christ my own.

Amazing love! how can it be
   That Thou, my God, shouldst die for me.

Look Up!

Glory in his holy name;
Let the hearts of those who seek the LORD rejoice.
Look to the LORD and his strength;
seek his face always.

1 CHRONICLES 16:10-11

Upward Gaze

Heavenly Father, You're a merciful God, never abandoning or destroying Your children. I praise You for being a faithful, loving God who allows Yourself to be found by those who seek You with all their heart and soul (Deuteronomy 4:29,31). Amen.

< MOM >

Donna poked her head inside her back door. "C'mon, Alex!" she called. "It's time to leave!" Moments later, nine-year-old Alex and her girlfriend giggled and ran out of the house toward the idling van. Rain splattered them; puddles muddied their sneakered feet.

"All aboard?" asked Doug as the girls climbed in. He stepped on the gas pedal and steered the vehicle onto the road. "Family camp or bust!"

Amid the girls' backseat chatter, Doug and Donna discussed this long-awaited vacation. They anticipated a refreshing time away from work and home responsibilities.

Before long, wind gusts pushed the van. Rain pelted the windshield. Doug adjusted the windshield wipers to a faster speed. "What's with this weather?" he asked. "Rain was forecast, but this is a major storm."

A couple of hours later, they approached the camp's vicinity. By now, the blackened sky hurled torrential rain across the highway. Trees twisted and snapped beside the road.

"We must be almost there," said Donna, staring out her window. "The camp pamphlet said a sign would be at the turnoff. I don't see anything yet, but it must be close."

Doug slowed the van, driving nearly ten miles as the womenfolk watched for the sign to no avail.

"Let's go back," suggested Donna. "Maybe we missed it." Ten miles yielded nothing. They retraced their path a third time. Nothing. Tornado-force winds threatened to blow their vehicle off the road.

"I don't understand," said Donna. "I know this is the right road. Maybe we should forget it and find a motel room. This isn't safe anymore." The others agreed. They drove several miles until they found a motel perched on the edge of a small town.

The next morning dawned bright and clear. The family climbed into their vehicle once more and traveled the same route. Within minutes, Donna spied the sign positioned high in a tree.

"Look! There it is," she said, laughing. "It was there the whole time. The storm made it difficult to see, but if we'd looked up, we would have seen it."

Their experience makes us chuckle and wonder why they didn't stop to ask directions. To that, Donna answers, "We thought we could find our own way." As a result, they wandered back and forth in a tornado, distracted by rain and wind, not thinking to look up.

Sound familiar? I've done it. Perhaps you have, too. We find ourselves in an emotional, physical, or spiritual storm. Like howling winds, fear and worry push and pull us. Simply staying on the road absorbs all our energies. Doubt clouds our vision. In our anxiety, we don't think to look up for direction.

If we look to the Lord, we find our questions answered. He's there all the time, whether we travel in sunshine or storm. He never leaves us. He walks beside us, never abandoning us to decipher life alone.

The next time you wonder if someone else could mother your children better than you, look up! When you worry about your kids' academic or social struggles, remember where your focus should be. If you're a single mom, weary from traveling the road alone, be encouraged—God is there to direct your path. He'll guide you to a place of rest and safety.

Look up, dear moms! May today's clouds part to reveal the Son's glorious presence in your life!

Inward Glimpse

Dear Father, thank You that You're always there for me. Help me remember to look up and not be distracted by stormy circumstances. Amen.

- When a storm surrounds you, where do you generally look for help—yourself? Friends? God? Write a prayer to the Lord, asking Him to help you look up before looking anywhere else for help.
- In today's "One More Peek," the Israelites were in big trouble. What was the remedy? This serpent represents Christ, who was lifted up on a cross. How are the two similar?

Outward Glance

Father, I pray that _____ will look to You and be radiant. May his face never be covered with shame. When he calls to You, please hear him and save him from all his troubles (Psalm 34:5-6). Thank You. Amen.

One More Peek

The people came to Moses and said, "We sinned when we spoke against the LORD and against you. Pray that the LORD will take the snakes away from us." So Moses prayed for the people. The LORD said to Moses, "Make a snake and put it up on a pole; anyone who is bitten can look at it and live." So Moses made a bronze snake and put it up on a pole. Then when anyone was bitten by a snake and looked at the bronze snake, he lived (Numbers 21:7-9).

Oh, My Stars!

*He determines the number of the stars and
calls them each by name. Great is our Lord and mighty in power;
his understanding has no limit.*
PSALM 147:4-5

Upward Gaze

Praise You for ever and ever, God, for creating the heavens. All wisdom and power are Yours. You give wisdom to the wise and knowledge to the discerning. You reveal deep and hidden things. You know what lies in the darkness, and light dwells with You (Daniel 2:20-22). Amen.

MOM

One crisp autumn evening, our family visited an amateur conservatory located in a stargazer's backyard. In addition to the huge telescope aimed at the sky through the dome-shaped roof, about a dozen smaller telescopes dotted the yard. Men, women, and children took turns identifying the planets and admiring heaven's jewels.

The nighttime sky fascinates mankind, and rightly so. Its immensity staggers the imagination. On a clear night we can see about 3000 stars glittering like diamonds hung on a black velvet curtain. A telescope with a three-inch diameter lens enhances the view to include about 600,000. That sounds like a lot until we discover that our galaxy contains about 200 billion stars. Astronomers estimate the total number of stars in the universe exceeds 200 billion billion.

My finite mind has difficulty wrapping itself around all those zeroes. Other mere mortals have struggled, too. Astronomers have tried to bring order to the universe's vastness by naming stars and defining their positions, but their limited knowledge restricts success. In several instances, ancient astronomers mistakenly transferred names from one star to another or assigned the wrong stars to constellations. And with multiple billions of stars out there, a person doesn't have to be a rocket scientist to figure out that man will never accurately map the limits of the universe.

God's creative handiwork leaves man's mind mystified. On the contrary, Scripture says God's understanding knows no limit. He not only knows the numbers of the stars but also calls them each by name. Imagine! Every one of those 200 billion billion stars has a personal identification code in God's books. They'll never be misplaced or confused with one another. In fact, because He created them, He knows every detail about them—their dimensions, their light-years from the earth, and the galaxy they call home.

Counting and naming the stars is easy for a God without restrictions. That fact should encourage our faith—God can accomplish this incredible feat, so doubting His wisdom is silly. And yet we do.

Our son or daughter struggles with a learning disability. We question, "Why *my* child?" Cancer strikes a little one. We cry out to God, "Do You know what You're doing?" Our teenager isn't accepted at the college or university of his choice. We ask, "Why not?"

We need to remember that viewing life from a mortal perspective is like surveying the night sky with the naked eye. The picture contains far more than we can imagine. Because we'll never, ever see all that God sees, He asks us to trust His wisdom.

God led men and women in the Bible through a variety of circumstances to teach them the principles of faith in Him alone. He does the same with us today. His ultimate goal is to perfect Jesus Christ's image in our lives, yet at the same time, He's accomplishing His overall plan in history.

The next time we question God's ways, we can be encouraged by looking at the night sky and remembering that His understanding is so infinite that He counts the stars and calls them by name. And if He can do that, we can trust His wisdom for our lives.

Inward Glimpse

Heavenly Father, I thank You for holding all wisdom in Your hand. Help me accept Your wisdom and rest in it. Amen.

- On a clear night, spread a blanket on the ground. Lie down alone or with your children and stargaze. Tell your children about the vastness of the universe and then remind them that God is even bigger.

- Write a prayer of praise to God for His wisdom in the midst of a confusing situation.

Outward Glance

Father, help _____ understand that You created the heavens and the earth. Help her appreciate that her breath comes from You, and You have called her in righteousness (Isaiah 42:5-6). Teach her that just as You've named the stars, You have called her by name, and she is Yours (Isaiah 43:1). Amen.

One More Peek

The heavens declare the glory of God;
the skies proclaim the work of his hands.
Day after day they pour forth speech;
night after night they display knowledge (Psalm 19:1-2).

Surprise!

How great are your works, O LORD,
how profound your thoughts!
PSALM 92:5

Upward Gaze

Heavenly Father, You are worthy of praise, for You form the mountains, create the wind, turn dawn to darkness, and tread earth's high places. You reveal Your thoughts to man (Amos 4:13). Your thoughts and ways are higher than mine (Isaiah 55:8). I trust them because you are the Lord God Almighty (Amos 4:13). Amen.

MOM

Beth and Steve stood beside the bathroom sink. They stared at the home pregnancy test, their eyes glued to the arrow pointing at the bright purple strip.

"This can't be," Steve stammered. He looked at his wife. "What are we going to do?"

"Have a baby," Beth answered numbly. She sat down on the edge of the bathtub and covered her face with her hands. "I can't believe this is happening. I'm nearly 45 years old. You're almost 47. We're old enough to be grandparents."

Steve stood silently, too shocked to respond. He and Beth enjoyed a great marriage and their two teenagers. They'd recently begun exploring options for empty-nest days ahead. But this...this would change everything.

The following days and weeks eased the initial shock. Together Steve and Beth thanked God for being in control of the pregnancy and asked Him for a healthy child. They recognized that He had a special purpose for trusting them with this surprise. They reminded themselves that children are a reward, a blessing from God. And they relaxed.

Beth grew excited as her body changed and she felt the baby's twitters. *What will this little one be like?* she wondered. *How will our teenagers relate to him or her? How will our family change?*

Rachel's birth answered Beth's questions. Their family's newest addition is a contented, easygoing child. The teenage siblings are crazy about their wee sister. Her arrival has knit their family together in a new way. Her giggles and coos produce joy and laughter. Her developmental achievements elicit cheers and applause.

Beth reflects on the past year and smiles. God's surprise brought challenges—trusting Him for a healthy baby after the doctor warned of high risks and offered an abortion, watching Beth's peers pursue their dreams while she set aside her nursing career again to return to diapers and long hours at home. But the blessings have been worth the sacrifices.

Beyond the challenges, God's surprise has produced new joy and wonder in Beth's life. She believes God blessed her and Steve for trusting His sovereignty throughout the pregnancy. She's enjoying a one-year maternity leave at home with her baby, and she has found a new ministry—encouraging young mothers with babies close to Rachel's age.

Beth and Steve's situation is a perfect example of how God occasionally surprises His children in ways they wouldn't choose for themselves. Beth says that, in a million years, she wouldn't have dreamt of becoming pregnant at age 44. But although she felt initial shock, her choice to accept God's plan brought tremendous joy. As she cuddles and nurses Rachel, she wouldn't exchange her circumstances for anything.

Sometimes God asks us to set aside our personal plans to embrace His. If we, like Beth and Steve, accept God's surprises as loving gifts rather than nuisances to our well-ordered lives, we too will experience joy. This acceptance is a matter of trust—believing that God loves us and has our best in mind. Believing that He knows what He's doing and doesn't make mistakes.

Has God given you an unexpected surprise recently? Perhaps you'll be moving to a new town or city soon. You wouldn't have chosen to do that, but God obviously has something else in mind. Maybe He's given you an unexpected responsibility at church or your child's school that wasn't in your blueprint.

Thank Him that He's in control, recognize that He has a special purpose, and relax. Watch in wonder at what He does, and enjoy His blessings!

Inward Glimpse

Dear Father, thank You for special surprises. Help me accept them as good gifts from a wise and loving Father's hand. Amen.

- Has God added surprises to your well-ordered life? If so, what are they?
- Read today's "One More Peek." Write a short prayer to God, asking Him to bring your desires into harmony with His.

Outward Glance

Father, I pray that _____ will trust in You at all times. When she doesn't understand your ways, may she pour out her heart to You. Be her refuge (Psalm 62:8). Make her glad by Your deeds. Teach her to sing for joy at the works of Your hands (Psalm 92:4). Amen.

One More Peek

Trust in the LORD and do good;
dwell in the land and enjoy safe pasture.

Delight yourself in the LORD
  and he will give you the desires of your heart.
Commit your way to the LORD
  trust in him and he will do this:
He will make your righteousness shine like the dawn,
  the justice of your cause like the noonday sun (Psalm
  37:3-6).

Monsters in the Dark

Have I not commanded you? Be strong and courageous.
Do not be terrified; do not be discouraged,
for the LORD your God will be with you wherever you go.
JOSHUA 1:9

Upward Glance

Father, You're the one who goes before me, fighting my battles and giving victory. The enemy looms large before me at times, but You're greater. Because You're with me, I won't be fainthearted or give way to panic (Deuteronomy 20:1-4). You're my fortress, my stronghold. You make wars cease to the ends of the earth. You break the bow and shatter the spear. You burn shields with fire. You'll be exalted among the nations, You'll be exalted in the earth (Psalm 46:8-11). Amen.

"Grace, would you please bring a jar of fruit from the basement?"

I hated that question! In reality, it was simple. Harmless. But every time Mom asked it, my seven-year-old imagination warned, *It's a death threat.* Terror played havoc with my thoughts. Visions of hairy, girl-eating monsters danced through my head. *I won't come back one of these days. I just know it! I'll vanish without a trace and no one will ever know what happened!*

Going downstairs was easy. I flicked the light switch and presto! The basement lit up. No monsters.

Then came the tough part. Before escaping from the dungeon, I had to turn off the basement light. Darkness enveloped me for a split second, making me easy prey for any monsters that might magically appear when the lights went off.

They're not going to catch me! I determined as I flew up the stairs two by two without a backward glance. I could feel the monsters' hot breath on my neck. I could hear their feet pounding behind me. I reached the top step—*safe!*—and stopped to catch my breath before entering the kitchen. I didn't want anyone to think I was a coward!

My vivid imagination tortured me, creating fear of nonexistent dangers. And it hasn't stopped. Even as an adult, I sometimes fear imaginary threats in the darkness of uncertainty, but I'm beginning to understand how to deal with them.

Less than four months after the terrorist attacks of September 11, our 18-year-old son, Matthew, left home to volunteer aboard a missionary ship for two years. He flew alone to Vancouver, British Columbia, and then to Minneapolis, Minnesota. From there he traveled to Amsterdam and finally to Frankfurt.

For 23 hours, my husband and I prayed for Matthew's safe journey, thanked the Lord that He was with him, and tracked his flights on the Internet. During that time, negative thoughts attacked. *What if Matt's luggage is lost? What if he misses a connecting flight? Worse yet, what if a terrorist boards his plane?*

Apprehension would have consumed me if I'd allowed it to dominate my mind. Instead, I mentally reviewed today's key verse and other similar Scriptures, and I bathed our home in praise and worship music.

Focusing on God's promises was like turning on a light. His Word chased away perceived monsters lurking in the dark corners of my vivid imagination. Confidence and courage replaced fear as I viewed the situation in the light of God's presence and power.

When health concerns, parenting challenges, marriage difficulties, or financial crises hound us, we're prone to hear the monsters of fear and worry pounding close behind. But whatever situation faces us, God's Word assures us that He is near and we need not fear. Instead, we can turn on the light! Fear and worry will vanish as we allow the rays of God's presence and promises to flood our souls with peace and joy.

Inward Glance

Heavenly Father, Your presence sheds light into the darkest recesses of my fearful heart. Help me to turn on the light when worry and apprehension threaten my confidence. I ask this in Jesus' name. Amen.

- What enemy looms before you right now? Write a prayer to God and thank Him for giving you victory. Write a Bible promise on a 3x5 card and post it where you'll see it often.

- Tell your children a story about an instance when you were afraid but God calmed or protected you.

Outward Glance

Heavenly Father, I pray that _____ will possess courage based on a solid knowledge of You and obedience to Your Word. May he be careful to obey Your commands fully, turning neither to the left nor the right, finding success wherever he goes (Joshua 1:6-9). May he recognize Your presence in his life. May he face life with strength and confidence, trusting Your promise to always be with him (Deuteronomy 31:8). Amen.

One More Peek

The LORD is my light and my salvation—
whom shall I fear?
The LORD is the stronghold of my life—
of whom shall I be afraid? (Psalm 27:1).

Muddy Feet

He lifted me out of the slimy pit,
out of the mud and mire;
he set my feet on a rock
and gave me a firm place to stand.
PSALM 40:2

Upward Gaze

I praise You, Father, for hearing me when I cry. You reached to me in love and pulled me from sin's grasp by Your mighty power and outstretched arm. You set me on the solid ground of Your everlasting love. May all who seek You rejoice and be glad in You; may those who love Your salvation always say, "The Lord be exalted!" (Psalm 40:16). Amen.

MOM

When I was five years old, my folks built a house in a new development. Construction surrounded us for several months after we moved in. Sidewalks and pavement didn't exist. Dump trucks, cement trucks, and other heavy equipment thundered past our door every day.

Young families populated the neighborhood, making it a playmate's paradise. But I faced one minor problem—most of my friends lived *across* the street. The geography of our neighborhood wasn't an issue in summer, fall, or winter. But when the snowy, southern Alberta winter thawed into slushy spring, it became a big deal, at least for little kids. The muddy road slopped and squished like chocolate pudding stirred several times a day by heavy trucks.

One afternoon I pulled on my lime green rubber boots to walk to a friend's house. I looked both ways before crossing the road, just as I'd been taught. Seeing no oncoming traffic, I stepped into the street. Within moments, mud covered my ankles. It sucked my feet deeper and deeper into its miry depths. I tried lifting my right foot, then my left, but it was hopeless. I couldn't move! I pulled. I twisted. I yanked. I jerked, all to no avail.

And then I heard a truck's deep roar. There it was—a cement truck looming on the horizon. It lumbered closer...closer. It looked big—very, very big.

Panic gripped me. *He doesn't see me!* I thought. *He's going to run over me!* I did the only thing I could do.

"Help!" I screamed. "Somebody help me!"

Mom came running. She slogged through the mud and put her hands under my armpits. She panted and pulled 'til I thought she was going to pull my arms off. As the cement truck idled nearby, she plucked me from my mucky grave and carried me to solid ground.

Life's like that sometimes, isn't it? We skip along our merry way until suddenly a problem grabs us. We struggle and fight and worry and stress, but we can't escape. About that time, another difficulty comes along, and maybe another. Like the cement truck, they loom larger and larger until we're convinced they're going to finish us off.

I faced this recently when Kim and I drove 1000 miles for my college homecoming and parents' fiftieth wedding anniversary celebration. Sure enough—the car died. It left us stranded by the highway in 95-degree heat until a tow truck arrived, and then it cost me $500 for repairs. That same day, I received news that a good friend had been killed in a car accident. A week later, after we'd returned home, my oven caught fire. I watched the flames lick their way around the upper element and cried, "Help!"

Always true to His Word, God rescued me. He plucked me from discouragement using Scripture to remind me of His unending love and faithfulness. He set my emotions and thoughts on the firm foundation of His hope and peace.

And as an extra-special bonus, He nudged a friend to give us a check for $500. That friend, by the way, knew nothing about the car repair bill. She and her husband just "felt" they should do this.

Is God good or what?

When we stand ankle-deep or even ear-deep in discouragement or worry, we can be encouraged by the fact that God knows all about our situation. He's standing by, just waiting for the invitation to help.

And our experience with life's muck and mire can make us more sensitive to someone else who needs to be rescued. Perhaps a phone call, a plate of freshly-baked cookies, a note, a hug, or a prayer would set that person's feet on solid ground today.

Inward Glimpse

Dear Father, thank You for rescuing me from discouragement and setting my feet on solid ground. Help me encourage others the same way. Amen.

- Any cement trucks bearing down on you today? One by one, give those problems to the Lord. Ask for wisdom to deal with them, and thank God for rescuing you.

- Write Psalm 40:2 on an index card and memorize it. Teach it to your children.

Outward Glance

Father, I thank You for hearing _____ when she calls out to You. When she's sinking in the muck and mire of discouragement or fear, lift her out and set her on solid ground. Put a new song in her mouth, a hymn of praise to You. Through Your working in her life, I pray that many will see and fear and put their trust in You (Psalm 40:2-3). Amen.

One More Peek

But I pray to you, O LORD,
    in the time of your favor;
in your great love, O God,
    answer me with your sure salvation.
Rescue me from the mire,
    do not let me sink....
Answer me, O LORD, out of the goodness of your love;
    in your great mercy turn to me (Psalm 69:13-14,16).

One Day at a Time

Therefore do not worry about tomorrow,
for tomorrow will worry about itself.
Each day has enough trouble of its own.
MATTHEW 6:34

Upward Gaze

Father, I sing of Your strength. In the morning I will sing of Your love. You are my fortress, my refuge in times of trouble. O my Strength, I sing praise to You. You are my loving God (Psalm 59:16-17). Your love goes with me every day. Thank You! Amen.

MOM

Eight-year-old Crystal tiptoed to the camp's kitchen door. Her chin quivered as she scanned the room for her aunt, a volunteer cook. The jovial, round-faced woman stood across the room, mixing cookie dough.

"Aunt Kathy," called Crystal softly. The woman glanced up.

"Crystal!" exclaimed Aunt Kathy. "I thought you went swimming with your counselor and the other kids. Do you need something?"

The girl couldn't answer. Tears spilled down her cheeks. A giant sob escaped her lips.

"Oh dear," exclaimed her aunt. She wiped her hands on her apron as she rushed to the door. Without a word, she hugged Crystal to her chest.

"What's wrong?" she asked. "Aren't you enjoying camp?"

"I'm having fun," said the girl. "I like my counselor and the other girls in my cabin."

"So, what's wrong?" pressed Aunt Kathy. She held Crystal's face in her hands and tipped her head. Their eyes met.

"I miss my mom and dad. I wanna go home. Please, can I go home?"

Aunt Kathy hugged Crystal again. She smoothed her hair, stalling for time as she pondered an appropriate answer. *What should I say? She feels overwhelmed, but she'll miss so much if she leaves. Perhaps focusing on one day at a time will make it easier.*

Finally she spoke. "It's okay to miss your mom and dad. I'm sure they miss you, too. But if you go home, you'll miss all the fun activities your counselor planned. Will you stay one more day? Tomorrow will seem easier."

Crystal sniffed and wiped her tears away. Staying one more day sounded better than staying all week. "Okay," she agreed. "I'll stay tomorrow."

Before she knew it, she'd survived a string of tomorrows. On the last day, her parents arrived to collect their daughter and her belongings. "Are you here already?" she asked. "I don't want to go home yet!"

Aunt Kathy overheard Crystal's remark and grinned, pleased that her advice had helped her niece enjoy her first summer camp experience.

Focus on one day at a time—wise instruction for us to remember, too, when we roll from bed on Monday morning facing the same problems or confronting the week's scribbled calendar. Each day contains an entry or two beyond the normal household or work responsibilities—dentist appointment, driving exam, basketball tournament, parent-teacher interviews, early morning band rehearsal, fund-raising car wash. Problems perplex us, and our schedule makes survival seem dubious.

We might not have an Aunt Kathy to embrace us, but we have a kind and compassionate heavenly Father to whom we can run when we're feeling stressed. He gives great counsel, too.

Today's key verse is an example: "Therefore do not worry about tomorrow, for tomorrow will worry about itself. Each day has enough trouble of its own." God gives that advice because He cares about our well-being. He knows anxiety weighs us down and harms our health.

He wants us to live life abundantly and not to be controlled by its demands.

We should step back when we feel anxious or burdened by the big picture. Perhaps we need to reevaluate priorities, plan more carefully, change or delete plans, or learn to live one day at a time. When we wake each morning, we can thank the Lord for the new day and commit it to Him before our feet hit the floor.

Before we know it, we'll be looking back on our week and asking, "The weekend is here already?"

Inward Glimpse

Dear Father, thank You for caring enough about me to give wise instruction about life. Help me remember to live one day at a time. Amen.

- If you're feeling swamped by your schedule, can you change something to ease the pressure? If so, what is it?
- Memorize this verse: "This is the day the LORD has made; let us rejoice and be glad in it" (Psalm 118:24). Commit to saying it before you get up each morning. Before long you'll notice a change in your perspective.

Outward Glance

Father, I pray that _____ will yearn for You every morning and every night. May Your name and renown be his heart's desire as he walks in the way of Your laws (Isaiah 26:8-9). May he seek to live each day, one day at a time, by the Holy Spirit's power. Amen.

One More Peek

This is the day the LORD has made;
let us rejoice and be glad in it.

O LORD, save us;
  O LORD, grant us success....
You are my God, and I will give you thanks;
  you are my God, and I will exalt you.
Give thanks to the LORD, for he is good;
  his love endures forever (Psalm 118:24-25,28-29).

Special Guest

For the LORD takes delight in his people;
he crowns the humble with salvation.
PSALM 149:4

Upward Gaze

Father, You're worthy of praise because You are filled with compassion. You delight to show mercy, You pardon sin, and You hurl all our iniquities into the depths of the sea (Micah 7:18-19). Praise You! Amen.

MOM

My friend Vikki has a four-year-old son who loves to play a simple game they call Guest. It goes like this:

Jordan exits their back door and runs around the house to the closed front door. He rings the bell and waits until Vikki answers with a cheery, "Hello, my guest! I'm so glad you've arrived. Would you like to come in?"

The little guy steps inside, grinning at the warm welcome. Vikki continues, "I hope you can stay awhile. Would you like a glass of water or milk? A cookie? Perhaps some crackers and peanut butter?" They proceed to the kitchen where mom pulls out a kitchen chair. "This is the best seat in the house—reserved especially for you!"

If Jordan worked hard to choose his clothing that morning, Vikki commends him. "Your clothes look so nice on you today, my guest. You made a fine choice!" If he's been especially happy, she might say, "It's so nice to see your smiling face!"

Jordan loves the attention. His mom's lavish hospitality surrounds him with the sense of being anticipated, accepted, and appreciated.

Vikki's response to Jordan resembles God's disposition toward us. He loves to spend time with His children, to enjoy fellowship without daily distractions. "I'm so glad you're here! I've been waiting for you," He says. "Can you stay awhile, or must you rush away?"

Understanding that concept has transformed my attitude toward my quiet time with God. I envision Him waiting eagerly for me by the front door like a best friend anticipating a good heart-to-heart. The thought makes me feel anticipated, accepted, and appreciated by the one who loves me more than I can imagine. No longer do I squeeze time into my schedule to read His Word and spend time in quiet prayer. Instead, I deliberately choose to set time aside to worship Him and enjoy His presence.

Vikki's response to Jordan teaches me another practical lesson. My kids are too old for playing preschool games now; we've moved into real-life teenage stuff, and my response toward them really matters.

How do I welcome them when they arrive home from school or work? How do I respond when they want to talk about their concerns? I must admit, I don't always greet them with enthusiasm. Sometimes I'm busy—if I'm writing against a deadline, I might just holler from my office, "How was your day?" and settle for a distant, "Fine." Sometimes I catch my thoughts a million miles away when I should be listening to my kids.

And how do my friends feel when they phone or drop by unexpectedly? Do I extend a gracious, "Hello, guest! Can you stay awhile?" Or do I brush them off with an excuse about why this is not a good time to visit?

I'm thankful God extends a gracious welcome to us anytime, day or night. He waits by the door for our arrival, ready to listen and talk.

Inward Glimpse

Father, thank You for welcoming me into Your presence anytime. Help me reflect that same response to my family and friends. Amen.

- Do you struggle with making yourself available to others? If so, in what way? What practical steps can you take to overcome that?
- Serve dinner by candlelight, using special dishes. Your kids may ask if guests are coming. Tell them you're serving dinner to some very special people—them.

Outward Glance

Heavenly Father, I pray that _____ will delight greatly in You. May his soul rejoice in You for clothing him in garments of salvation and a robe of righteousness. As he spends time in Your presence, may he come to know You as the God who exercises kindness, justice, and righteousness on earth (Jeremiah 9:24). Amen.

One More Peek

The LORD your God is with you,
  he is mighty to save.
He will take great delight in you,
  he will quiet you with his love,
  he will rejoice over you with singing (Zephaniah 3:17).

Kid Keeper

I always pray with joy...being confident of this,
that he who began a good work in you
will carry it on to completion until the day of Christ Jesus.
PHILIPPIANS 1:4,6

Upward Gaze

Heavenly Father, I praise You because You are able to keep Your children from falling and to present them before Your glorious presence without fault and with great joy. You are the only God and Savior, full of glory, majesty, power, and authority through Jesus Christ, now and forever! (Jude 24). Amen.

MOM

Sue stood on her front steps and watched her son and daughter climb into their dad's truck. *This isn't the way I'd planned to raise my children,* she thought. *I never thought divorce would happen to me.*

Back in the kitchen, she glanced at the calendar. Its scribbled notes reminded her of the custody agreement she and her ex had made several months earlier. The kids bounced back and forth between households—one week with him and his new family, the next with her.

In practical terms, the arrangement worked well. When Sue's work schedule required night shifts, the kids lived with their father. Her days off fell during the weeks the kids stayed with her, freeing her to give them undivided attention.

The agreement gave both parents equal time with the children, but one issue concerned Sue. She took them to Sunday school and church, but her ex refused to do likewise. She tried her best to instill godly values into the children's lives, but their father's home held different standards.

When the children were younger, relatively minor issues surfaced. But now the kids were approaching their teen years, and Sue's concerns increased. Her children's older step-siblings listened to music and watched videos she considered unacceptable. Their dress standards bothered her. Though Sue's kids weren't old enough to date, she cringed at the thought of potential battles lurking in the near future. She could almost hear the kids—*So-and-so can date at 15. Dad says I can, too.* She hoped they would seek involvement in their church youth group, but she worried about the possibility of sporadic attendance. *If they attend only twice a month, will they lose interest?*

Sue discussed her concerns with close friends and prayer partners. "My children belong to two families who differ on almost everything," she confided. "I worry about the negative effects of inconsistencies, of double standards. How will the kids learn to do what's right when their parents don't agree? I can't supervise their behavior when they're at their dad's house. I can't be there to watch out for them and help them make wise choices."

Her friends sympathized. Together they prayed regularly for God's protection over the children's hearts and minds. They asked God to be their refuge, their source of wisdom, their Rock. They believed He would instill a love for His written Word within them and give them a desire to follow Jesus wholeheartedly.

Sue's story hasn't ended yet. The custody sharing continues, and so do the prayers. When Sue becomes anxious, she reminds herself that God is able to keep her children with or without her help. She knows that because both children have received Jesus Christ as their Savior, the Holy Spirit lives in them and will guide and teach them.

Perhaps you face similar circumstances—two families with different values raise your children. Perhaps you're a single mom raising a family alone, worried about your kids' spiritual and emotional development, especially since you can't always be there for them. Perhaps your situation is different—your teens are in high school or away at college, and you worry about their ability to live by godly standards in a secular society.

Whatever your situation, be encouraged. The heavenly Father watches your children. If they have chosen to follow Jesus Christ, His Spirit lives within them and will teach them to walk in truth, convict them when they disobey, and guide their decisions. He can keep their hearts with or without our presence. Nothing limits His resources to get the job done, whatever their ages.

Perhaps He'll bring an enthusiastic, wise Christian teacher into their lives, or maybe a godly employer, roommate, or coach. Maybe they'll develop positive friendships and spend time in other homes that reinforce your values.

Continue praying for your children and entrusting them to the Lord. May you see Him answer in amazing ways!

Inward Glimpse

Dear Father, thank You for loving my children. Help me entrust them to Your care. Amen.

- What concerns you most about your children's spiritual, emotional, mental, or physical development? Write your concerns out.

- Write a prayer in which you commit those concerns to the Lord, recognizing Him as the one to whom you can entrust your children's souls.

Outward Glance

Father, I pray that you will fill _____ with the knowledge of Your will in all spiritual wisdom and understanding. May he live a life pleasing to You in every way, bearing fruit in every good work and growing in the knowledge of God (Colossians 1:9-10). Amen.

One More Peek

And this is my prayer: that your love may abound more and more in knowledge and depth of insight, so that you may be able to discern what is best and may be pure and blameless until the day of Christ, filled with the fruit of righteousness that comes through Jesus Christ—to the glory and praise of God (Philippians 1:9-11).

Heavenly Lemonade

And we know that in all things
God works for the good of those who love him,
who have been called according to his purpose.
ROMANS 8:28

Upward Gaze

Father, You're worthy of praise because You are sovereign. You can do all things—no purpose of Yours can be thwarted (Job 42:2). You do whatever You desire and perform what You have decreed for me (Job 23:13-14). I trust You, for You're able to turn difficulties into something good. Amen.

God makes awesome lemonade from life's sour circumstances. I've witnessed the process personally several times. One instance began with a building contractor's words: "Sure, no problem. Your house will be complete before school begins in September. Don't worry—you'll move in by the end of August."

Whew! That timing was crucial to me. We'd recently sold our home and had to move out by the end of June. We could live with Gene's folks until the new house was complete. But there was one hitch—they lived nearly an hour's drive from our children's new school. If the house wasn't finished by early September, the kids and I would have to fight freeway rush-hour traffic twice a day. I was up to my eyeballs in stress already. I didn't want more.

Construction began. The house grew from foundation to framework. In early August, however, progress ground to a halt. After two weeks with no builders on-site, I knew the completion date wouldn't be met. My attitude nosedived. Frustrated, I phoned the contractor.

"What's happening?" I asked.

"The drywallers have been tied up on another job," he explained.

"Will the house be ready at the end of the month like you said?"

He laughed. I cried.

Gene and I prayed for a solution to our dilemma. A few days later, a close family friend asked about the building project. We explained our situation. "Would you consider house-sitting for me for two weeks?" he asked. "If your house isn't finished by the time I return, you're welcome to stay longer." His home sat only ten minutes from school. Our prayers were answered!

The first day of school dawned. As the kids and I waited at the bus stop, another family joined us. "Hi, I'm Wendy," said the mom. "Welcome to the neighborhood. We're your closest neighbors." We chatted briefly, and then she extended an invitation. "A Moms in Touch group prays for our school. Would you like to join us?"

Moms in Touch? I'd never heard of it, but Wendy's explanation of praying Scripture for our children whet my appetite. I participated and eventually led the group for the next several years until we moved to Canada.

My involvement with Moms in Touch changed my life. Although filling my mind with Scripture didn't make me a perfect mom, it placed my focus on the living God rather than circumstances, convicted me of sin, supplied wisdom for parenting, and taught me to pray according to God's will.

Ten years ago, life tasted sour when our house wasn't finished according to my schedule. But God squeezed the lemons and added a heaping helping of sweet loving-kindness, resulting in major spiritual growth in my life.

Scripture says that God is able to make all things work together for the good of those who love Him and are called according to His purpose.

Tragic or trying circumstances don't stump God. He weaves them together and forms a tapestry of exquisite beauty.

He made lemonade from Paul and Silas' prison experience way back in New Testament days, too. Prison chains held the Gospel-preaching duo, but God used their sentence as an opportunity to show His power to the warden, who committed his life to following Jesus Christ.

When bitter circumstances surround us, God can and will use them for our good and His glory. We wonder how that's possible when we're weary from caring for a special-needs child or rebellious teenager, when we're exhausted from trying to help our family adjust to a new location, or when we're discouraged from chronic fatigue or illness.

God's recipe always works. When we give Him the lemons and trust Him to add a hefty dose of His loving-kindness, He always turns our experience into something good for us and glorious for Himself.

Inward Glimpse

Dear Father, thank You for turning sour circumstances into something good. Help me to remember that You're able and to watch with anticipation as You work. Amen.

- What sour circumstances are you facing or have you faced recently?
- Write a prayer to God and ask Him to make lemonade!

Outward Glance

Father, I pray that when _____ encounters difficulties, he will maintain his righteousness (Job 27:6). When circumstances discourage him, may he remember that You know the way he takes. When You test him, bring him forth as pure gold (Job 23:10). Amen.

One More Peek

About midnight Paul and Silas were praying and singing hymns to God, and the other prisoners were listening to them. Suddenly there was such a violent earthquake that the foundations of the prison were shaken. At once all the prison doors flew open, and everybody's chains came loose (Acts 16:25-26).

A Mighty Fortress

*He who fears the LORD has a secure fortress,
and for his children it will be a refuge.*
PROVERBS 14:26

Upward Gaze

God, in the morning I will sing of Your strength and love,
for You are my fortress, my refuge in times of trouble. O my
Strength, I sing praise to You, my fortress and my loving God
(Psalm 59:16-17). Amen.

◄ MOM ►

"Wow!" I whispered as I opened the window blinds. Freshly fallen
snow blanketed our lawn and coated the trees' bare branches. Large wet
flakes floated lazily from the gray sky.

Seconds later, our pajama-clad kids charged into the bedroom. "Is
there school today?" asked Matt. We turned on the radio and listened,
fingers crossed, as the announcer listed closures. Sure enough, he named
our district.

"Yahoo!" the kids shouted. They gobbled hot oatmeal and then
donned parkas, ski pants, mitts, and boots and dashed outside. Before
long, the yard featured angel prints, fox-and-goose trails, and a snow-
man complete with a plaid scarf, stick arms, and a carrot nose.

The threesome admired their artwork, and then Matt suggested
another idea. "Let's build forts!" They formed two three-foot-high walls
facing each other about 20 feet apart. Matt hid behind one with his
snowball arsenal; the girls hid behind the other with theirs.

The battle began. White bombs pelted the forts and exploded on impact. Missiles soared over the walls and clobbered the enemy, who spewed threats of revenge. Laughter and screams filled the air until someone yelled, "Cease-fire!"

Silence reigned for a few moments. Then, without warning, a stray bomb plastered its victim's back. Combat resumed until steaming hot chocolate wooed the warriors indoors.

Later that day I contemplated the fort's melted remains. *Not very strong,* I thought. *Not at all like real fortresses.*

While in college, I visited an authentic European fortress that was built in the Middle Ages. A tour guide explained that such structures were difficult to capture for several reasons. Their mountaintop or hillside perch secured an unhindered view of the surrounding area. Approaching armies could be seen for miles, giving guards and soldiers ample time to prepare for battle. Stone walls were up to 33 feet thick, offering protection from enemy attacks, weather, and fire. Often, additional defenses such as fortified courtyards and moats encased the inner tower that housed the inhabitants.

When I read Scripture that describes God as a fortress, I draw a mental picture of the European castle. I imagine myself dwelling safely in the inner tower, surrounded by moats and courtyards and immense stone walls. Even though battles rage outside, I'm hidden from danger, able to carry on without worry or fear because God Himself protects me.

This doesn't mean I'll never face problems or trials, but it *does* mean that God will protect me in the midst of them.

This holds true for my children, too. I know they'll encounter difficulties in their lifetime. God may allow severe testing or call them into missionary careers in dangerous countries. Rather than be anxious, however, I remember that He is their fortress.

Three months after 9/11, Matthew, 18, flew to Germany alone to board an oceangoing missionary ship. As his departure date approached, several well-meaning individuals asked, "Aren't you afraid to let him go? There's so much political unrest. There's a war happening. Aren't you scared?"

I answered, "No, I'm not fearful. Matt's following God's call on his life. There's no safer place than in the center of His will." My response wasn't based on a naive view of the world's precarious state. It was based on the firm conviction that God was Matt's fortress amid the uncertainty.

Perhaps one of the greatest gifts we can give our children is the confidence—the fearlessness—that comes from knowing God as their fortress. We must possess it ourselves before we can pass it on to them. By filling our minds with thoughts of God as our fortress, we'll experience victory when worry or fear stomp into our territory and threaten to conquer.

Inward Glimpse

Dear Father, thank You for being my fortress. Help me rest in You, free from worry or fear. Amen.

- Describe what having God as your fortress means to you.
- Read the hymn, "A Mighty Fortress Is Our God" on the next page. Which stanza means the most to you, and why?

Outward Glance

Father, I pray that _____ will acknowledge You as her rock, her fortress, her deliverer. Be her shield and the horn of her salvation, her stronghold. May she call on You because You're worthy of praise, and may she be saved from her enemies (Psalm 18:1-3). Amen.

One More Peek

He who dwells in the shelter of the Most High
will rest in the shadow of the Almighty.
I will say of the LORD, "He is my refuge and my fortress,
my God, in whom I trust" (Psalm 91:1-2).

A Mighty Fortress
Is Our God

Martin Luther

A mighty fortress is our God,
    A bulwark never failing;
Our helper He, amid the flood
    Of mortal ills prevailing.
For still our ancient foe doth seek to work us woe;
His craft and power are great, and, armed with cruel hate,
On earth is not his equal.

Did we in our own strength confide,
    Our striving would be losing,
Were not the right Man on our side,
    The Man of God's own choosing.
Dost ask who that may be? Christ Jesus, it is He;
Lord Sabaoth His name, from age to age the same,
And He must win the battle.

And though this world, with devils filled,
    Should threaten to undo us,
We will not fear, for God hath willed
    His truth to triumph through us.
The prince of darkness grim—we tremble not for him;
His rage we can endure, for lo! his doom is sure,
One little world shall fell him.

It's Only a House

Do not worship any other god, for the LORD,
whose name is Jealous, is a jealous God.
EXODUS 34:14

Upward Gaze

Heavenly Father, there is none like You. You revealed Yourself to the Israelites long ago, taking them from Egypt by testings, by miraculous signs and wonders, by war, and by a mighty hand and an outstretched arm. With great and awesome deeds You showed Yourself so they would know that You are God, and above You there is no other. I praise You because You are the same today—the true God (Deuteronomy 4:34-35). Your deeds are still great and awesome today. You are exalted above all else. Amen.

◄ MOM ►

"Give up your dream house and move to Canada?" Several friends shook their heads in disbelief at our decision. They knew the obstacles we'd overcome to get construction permits to build on prime lakefront property only four years earlier. They knew the pleasure we'd received from inviting friends to swim and water-ski at our home. Many had participated in impromptu potlucks on the lawn or marshmallow roasts around an evening campfire. This custom-built house had accommodated relatives and strangers, missionaries, and our children's friends. Now God was asking us to give it up.

A few months earlier, my husband and I sensed God's leading us to work at a Christian camp in Canada. Financially, selling the house was a necessity. Committed to obeying His call upon our lives, we listed our home with a Realtor.

One afternoon was particularly difficult for Stephanie and Kim as moving day approached. Sitting by the large dining room window, they cried, "How can we leave this place? Our bedroom is so pretty! We don't want to leave the lake!"

Twelve-year-old Matthew put it in perspective. "It's just a house, and it could burn down tomorrow," he stated matter-of-factly. He was right.

What might have happened if we'd refused to go because of a strong attachment to the house? We can only speculate. Perhaps our children would have missed the opportunity to meet their new friends, we wouldn't be involved in camp ministry, and we wouldn't have seen God provide for our needs in amazing ways.

God desires our complete allegiance, and He deserves it! After all, He gave up His only Son to die for our sins in order to draw us into a right relationship with Himself.

We have to be on our guard, however. Our culture tosses many pretty things our way, trying to lure our affection away from God. A fancy house, a stylish wardrobe, an expensive car, a position high up the corporate ladder, a fat retirement account—all are modern-day false gods. Even pursuing a good reputation as a fantastic housekeeper or super-mom can be a false god.

By reading the Word, practicing God's presence moment by moment in our lives, and cultivating an attitude of thanksgiving and praise, we'll keep our hearts where they should be—set on the only true God.

Inward Glimpse

Dear Father, thank You for investing your Son's life in me. Keep me true to You. Help me not to be drawn away by any false gods. I love You. Amen.

- Have you allowed false gods in your life? If so, what are they? Write a prayer to God and ask Him to help you get rid of these gods and restore your relationship with Him.
- Meditate on the hymn, "Jesus Calls Us" on the next page. Which stanza means the most to you, and why?

Outward Glance

Father, I pray that _____ will not make an idol out of anything in heaven above or in the waters below. May he bow down in his heart to You alone, recognizing You as a jealous God. Teach him that others are affected by his decisions and priorities. May he understand that You punish the children for the sin of the fathers to the third and fourth generation of those who hate You, but You show Your love to thousands who love You and keep Your commandments (Deuteronomy 5:8-10). Amen.

One More Peek

Acknowledge and take to heart this day that the LORD is God in heaven above and on the earth below. There is no other. Keep his decrees and commands, which I am giving you today, so that it may go well with you and your children after you and that you may live long in the land the LORD your God gives you for all time (Deuteronomy 4:39-40).

Jesus Calls Us

Cecil F. Alexander

Jesus calls us; o'er the tumult
  Of our life's wild, restless sea,
Day by day His sweet voice soundeth,
  Saying, "Christian, follow Me."

Jesus calls us from the worship
  Of the vain world's golden store,
From each idol that would keep us,
  Saying, "Christian, love Me more."

In our joys and in our sorrows,
  Days of toil and hours of ease,
Still He calls, in cares and pleasures,
  "Christian, love Me more than these."

Jesus calls us: by Thy mercies,
  Savior, may we hear Thy call,
Give our hearts to Thine obedience,
  Serve and love Thee best of all.

Baseball Caps and Other Stuff

Every good and perfect gift is from above,
coming down from the Father of the heavenly lights,
who does not change like shifting shadows.
JAMES 1:17

Upward Gaze

Heavenly Father, I praise You because You answer prayer and grant my heart's desire. You meet me with the blessings of good things; You set a crown of gold upon my head. You've given me the best gift of all—eternal life through Jesus Christ (Psalm 21:2-4). Amen.

"God is too busy with big stuff like wars and floods and famines to care about our petty concerns."

Ever heard that statement? I have, and I disagree. God *does* care about our little concerns. I've witnessed the evidence.

When we lived in Washington state, we attended one or two professional baseball games each year. Because tickets taxed our family budget, we bypassed stadium snacks and souvenirs. If the kids wanted a game memento, they spent their own money.

One evening, enroute to a game, Matthew and Stephanie sported their favorite team's baseball caps, which they purchased the previous season. Kim envied their headgear.

"Please, can I have a cap, too?" she begged.

"Did you bring your own money?" asked Gene.

"No."

"Then you'll have to wait until next time."

"But Dad…" she moaned.

Later that evening, the two ball teams battled for victory. The pitcher pitched…the batter swung…*crack!* The ball soared toward outer space. Forty-five thousand cheering fans jumped to their feet. And as they did, a baseball cap fluttered from somewhere above us and landed squarely in our space. Gene picked it up and looked around, hoping to find its owner. No one claimed it. Kim had her hat.

"The baseball cap from heaven," we dubbed it.

Stephanie received her own special gift from above recently. Spending three weeks in an overseas ministry opportunity meant missing her favorite music group's concert in another town. A few weeks after she returned, the group performed in our church! Our town sits on the extreme left side of the map, far off anyone's concert route. Steph even enjoyed a personal chat with the musicians in the parking lot.

Does God care about the little things? Yes, indeed. Here's one more evidence: Matthew was only two years old when we purchased a home and he gained his own bedroom. I thought wallpaper would make his room more inviting.

"What pictures would you like on your walls?" I asked him.

"Cars and boats and trains and airplanes," my toddler replied matter-of-factly.

That's awfully specific, I thought, but God came through again—cars, boats, trains, and airplanes. Some people might call that a coincidence. I call it evidence that God loves toddlers enough to care about the things they care about.

Why does God care about the little things? He cares because He delights in His children and receives glory when we acknowledge His gifts. When we've experienced blessings like this, Gene and I have always been careful to say, "Wow! See what God did? He answered our prayers!"

As a result, our children understand that God, the King of the universe, is personally interested in them.

They also understand that He doesn't give them everything they want. Sometimes He says no. But often He delights to bless them with little things.

Situations such as our family has experienced provide delightful teaching opportunities for kids of every age. They also provide encouragement at a later date if we record them in a journal.

We can keep our eyes open for opportunities to bless others, too. I enjoy making cards or buying small gifts on sale—purse-sized hand creams or notebooks, mugs, stationery sets, candles—and stashing them for friends who need a pick-me-up. Encouraging notes tucked in a lunchbox or left on a pillow let other people know that regardless of how busy we are, they're in our thoughts.

May you enjoy a special little blessing today!

Inward Glimpse

Dear Father, thank You for being mindful of my small concerns. Make me mindful of other people's concerns. Amen.

- Have you enjoyed one of God's little blessings recently? What was it?
- What concern do you have that seems too minor for God? Write it down and commit it to Him.

Outward Glance

Father, I pray that You will grant _____'s heart's desire and fulfill all your counsel in his life (Psalm 20:4-5 NASB). Teach him to pray according to Your will, and open his eyes to recognize Your answers (1 John 5:14). Amen.

One More Peek

Ask and it will be given to you; seek and you will find; knock and the door will be opened to you. For everyone who asks receives; he who seeks finds; and to him who knocks, the door will be opened....If you, then, though you are evil, know how to give good gifts to your children, how much more will your Father in heaven give good gifts to those who ask him! (Matthew 7:7-8,11).

The Tree House

The eternal God is your refuge,
and underneath are the everlasting arms.
DEUTERONOMY 33:27

Upward Gaze

Lord, You have been our dwelling place through all generations. Before the mountains were born or You brought forth the earth and the world, from everlasting to everlasting You are God (Psalm 90:1-2). You are my strong refuge. My mouth is filled with Your praise, declaring your splendor all day (Psalm 71:7-8). Amen.

MOM

"Daddy, can you build us a tree house?" Kim asked a few days after we moved to the camp. "Steph and I really want a place to hide."

Gene agreed. The move from Washington to British Columbia had been difficult for the kids. They'd left everything familiar behind—friends, relatives, home, church, and school. Building a tree house together could be a great stress reliever. And the completed project could provide a fun play space or, as Kim termed it, a hiding place.

Gene and the girls selected an appropriate fir tree, pulled lumber from a scrap woodpile, and began construction. Several hours later, they stopped hammering and surveyed their work.

Perched amidst strong branches, the teeny house formed a secure retreat. Its walls, roof, and windows kept out rain and four-legged furry forest friends. Carpet squares covered the wooden floor—a padded place for avid readers to stretch out with a good book or for giggly girls to toss down sleeping bags at night. It was perfect—a quiet place, their own space, a refuge specially suited to help them rise above the stress in their lives.

Sometimes moms need a refuge, too. Early mornings and late nights weary us. Juggling busy schedules wears on us. Society's frantic pace leaves us breathless, feeling trapped on a treadmill that's stuck on "fast." If we don't slow down and set aside time for quiet reflection, spiritual refreshment, physical exercise, and social interaction, we may become frustrated, fed-up, and furious—a volcano waiting to blow!

Where can we find refuge from life's pressures? Tree houses may or may not work, depending on the door size! Perhaps a bedroom or den offers sanctuary. Maybe a backyard vegetable garden, a park bench, a sandy beach, a favorite coffee shop, or a chair on the deck. Maybe an annual women's retreat. Physical locations vary from mom to mom.

Sometimes we don't have the luxury of seeking quiet refuge. Our children are young and demand constant attention. A physically or mentally challenged child requires round-the-clock care. A single mom has neither time nor resources to escape.

Regardless of circumstances, we share a mutual spiritual refuge—God. Scripture says He's our eternal refuge, He's always there for us. At any time of day or night, we can run to Him and hide. He shelters us from discouragement, fear, and worry, and offers quiet peace instead.

In fact, according to Strong's concordance, the word *refuge* in today's key verse implies something stronger than a temporary retreat. It implies a dwelling place, like an animal's den or a person's home.

In other words, God, our refuge, wants us to dwell permanently in His presence—moment by moment, day by day. He wants us to find our security and pleasure in Him at all times, not only when we need our spiritual batteries recharged.

When we make Him our refuge, we rise above the stress in our lives. The circumstances might not change, but our perspective will be characterized by hope and joy rather than dejection and despair.

Inward Glimpse

Dear Father, thank You for being my refuge. Teach me to dwell in Your presence. Amen.

- How can you make your home a welcome refuge for others?
- Write a prayer of thanks to God for being your refuge at all times and not only in crisis.

Outward Glance

Father, I pray that _____ will take refuge in you. Rescue her and deliver her in Your righteousness. Never let her be put to shame (Psalm 71:1-2). Be her refuge, a strong tower against the foe. May she long to dwell in Your tent forever and find refuge in the shelter of Your wings (Psalm 61:3-4). Amen.

One More Peek

If you make the Most High your dwelling—
*   even the LORD, who is my refuge—*
then no harm will befall you,
*   no disaster will come near your tent.*
For he will command his angels concerning you
*   to guard you in all your ways;*
they will lift you up in their hands,
*   so that you will not strike your foot against a stone*
(Psalm 91:9-12).

Neon Confessions

*The LORD searches every heart and
understands every motive behind the thoughts.*
1 CHRONICLES 28:9

Upward Gaze

Heavenly Father, I praise You because You alone are holy; there is no Rock like You (1 Samuel 2:2). You are my help and my shield; therefore, I hope in You. In You my heart rejoices, for I trust in Your holy name (Psalm 33:20-21). You have ascended amid shouts of joy! You have risen amid the sounding of trumpets! I sing praises to You, my King. You are King of all the earth, and I sing a psalm of praise to Your holy name (Psalm 47:5-7). Amen.

MOM

"Hey, Mom!" called Kim, bouncing into the room. "You know what I used to think?" I was unprepared for the dynamic tidbit of truth that followed. "I used to think my head had a neon sign stuck on it to show my thoughts. I had to be really careful because other people would know what I was thinking."

As if that wasn't enough to cause shivers, she continued. "If people weren't there to read the sign, a loudspeaker blared my thoughts!"

That would be an effective way to keep my thought life in check! My imagination raced. I pondered what the previous Sunday would have been like if Kim's neon signs were real. I pictured myself sitting sanctimoniously in my pew, my eyes fixed on the pulpit. Meanwhile, flashing messages on the back of my head shocked those behind me— *Anne would look great if she lost about thirty pounds...I hope the pastor keeps his sermon short so we can go home early...Helen's new outfit must have cost a small fortune. How can she afford it?*

I shuddered and thought about my thoughts earlier that morning. How would my family feel if a loudspeaker suddenly blared, "I don't have time for prayer this morning—too many things to get done around the house! If I hear one more complaint about the food, I'm outta here! If I want something done right, I have to do it myself!"

Conviction was instant and pointed. My heart attitude needed a complete makeover before my thoughts could please God. I confessed my sin, asking Him to exchange pride for humility, to replace bitterness with forgiveness. I prayed for contentment rather than jealousy and compassion instead of criticism.

Falling into a pattern of negative thinking is easy, especially when we're tired or discouraged. Others may not know what we're thinking, but God does. He searches hearts and understands every intent of the thoughts. Outward actions might be commendable, but He knows our motives.

How can we keep our thoughts pleasing to the Lord Jesus, our perfect example? By thinking on things that are pure, worthy of praise, and honoring to Him. When we find ourselves slipping into negative thinking patterns, we can confess our sin and thank Jesus for His forgiveness.

We must preserve our thoughts so our sign flashes messages of God's love and light, healing and peace, truth and splendor to those around us. And when we do so, we please God, the holy one who knows our deepest thoughts.

Inward Glimpse

Heavenly Father, I trust Your ability to keep me from falling into negative thinking patterns. Make every aspect of my life model Jesus Christ. I love You. Amen.

- If a neon sign flashed your thoughts, could you stay in the room, or would you have to run for cover? Thank God for forgiveness and a fresh start. Hum or sing a favorite chorus or hymn as you work today.

- In his book *My Utmost for His Highest,* Oswald Chambers says,

> Is there a thought in your heart about which you would not like to be dragged into the light? Renounce it as soon as it springs up; renounce the whole thing until there is no hidden thing of dishonesty or craftiness about you. Envy, jealousy, strife—these things arise not necessarily from the disposition of sin, but from the make-up of your body which was used for this kind of thing in days gone by. Maintain a continual watchfulness so that nothing of which you would be ashamed arises in your life.[5]

Write a prayer in which you ask God to help you maintain that watchfulness.

Outward Glance

Father, I pray that _____ will live a blameless life, trusting You without wavering. Keep Your loving-kindness before her eyes. Help her walk continually in Your truth (Psalm 26:1,3). I pray that she will be sensitive to Your Holy Spirit, inviting You to search her heart, revealing any hurtful way. Lead her in the everlasting way (Psalm 139:23-24). May she put away any false god or teaching and yield her heart to You (Joshua 24:23). Amen.

One More Peek

Therefore, prepare your minds for action; be self-controlled; set your hope fully on the grace to be given you when Jesus Christ is revealed. As obedient children, do not conform to the evil desires you had when you lived in ignorance. But just as he who called you is holy, so be holy in all you do; for it is written: "Be holy, because I am holy" (1 Peter 1:13-16).

Garden Seeds

He who began a good work in you will carry it on to completion until the day of Christ Jesus.
PHILIPPIANS 1:6

Upward Gaze

There is none like You, Lord. No deeds can compare with Yours. All the nations will worship before You and bow before Your name. You are great and do marvelous deeds; You alone are God (Psalm 86:8-10). I praise Your holy name with my innermost being (Psalm 103:1). Amen.

MOM

I followed instructions religiously: Pulled chickweed. Raked soil lightly. Laid a bed of peat moss. Spread flower seeds. Added fertilizer. Raked lightly again. Rolled to press the seeds firmly in the soil.

Then I waited. So did my family. We authored a new proverb—"A watched flower garden never blooms." It's true. Every morning for three weeks I peeked through the blinds at the garden patch below and was greeted with—nothing.

Finally a greenish tint covered the garden. "It's happening!" I shouted. "The flowers! They're here!" My kids jumped up from the breakfast table and flew to the window for their first glimpse of new beginnings. Sure enough, green poked through the soil, responding to spring sunshine.

I checked my floral babies every morning. As they grew stronger and taller, however, they adopted an all-too-familiar appearance. I denied my fears as long as possible but then succumbed to the awful truth. My babies weren't flowers at all!

"That's it!" I told my husband, Gene. "I'm declaring chickweed war. I'll show no mercy." I bought a roll of black plastic. If I covered the entire garden, perhaps the weeds would die in the winter months. Next spring we would plant grass. So much for wildflower fantasies.

I dragged the plastic roll to the garden. *Good try,* I consoled myself. *Oh well. Grass and a raised perennial bed will be pretty, too.* And then I saw it. A lupine—tiny, buried in the chickweed. There was another. And another! *Forget the plastic!* I thought. *I'll return it and get my money back!*

I stopped right there and prayed, "God, You're the Creator. You designed flowers in the beginning; they show Your glory. Please bless this garden with blooms for others to enjoy. Thank You."

God answered. While I picked weeds, the garden exploded into an ever-changing color palette. Red poppies. Pink lupines. Black-eyed Susans. White daisies. Blue and purple bachelor buttons, and more!

God—omnipotent Creator—brought forth a 500-square-foot flower garden from a few handfuls of tiny seeds. Amazing! After planting, watering, and weeding, I could do nothing to produce blossoms. Only God could do that.

My flower bed reminds me of parenting. We try to do everything right—read how-to books about raising healthy kids, teach good manners, attend parent-teacher conferences, monitor the TV, have family devotions, and pray.

Sometimes we marvel at the emotional and spiritual development in our children's lives. Other days we throw our hands in the air, wondering if they'll ever grow up. As much as we'd like to, we can't force their development.

God loves our children infinitely more than we ever could. We must parent to the best of our ability and, though it may be difficult, take our hands off to let God accomplish His good purpose in their lives. Only He, through His Holy Spirit, can produce the growth He desires, conforming them to the image of Jesus Christ.

Inward Glimpse

Heavenly Father, thank You for loving my children and desiring to conform them to Christ's image. May they grow up to show Your glory. Help me to trust You in the process. I ask this in Jesus' name. Amen.

- What character qualities are you trusting God to produce in your children's lives?
- What qualities does He want to produce in you as a mom? Ask Him to cleanse any undesirable qualities from your life, replacing them with the fruit of the Spirit.

Outward Glance

Father, You've set a choice before _____. Work in her heart so she'll choose life and blessings. Because You are life, I pray that she will love You, listen to Your voice, and hold fast to You (Deuteronomy 30:19-20). Cause her to walk in the way of righteousness, for in that path is life and immortality (Proverbs 12:28). Help her lead a blameless life with a blameless heart. Help her set before her eyes no vile thing. May she sing Your praise forever (Psalm 101:1-3). Amen.

One More Peek

But the fruit of the Spirit is love, joy, peace, patience, kindness, goodness, faithfulness, gentleness and self-control (Galatians 5:22-23).

Attitude Check

Each of you should look not only to your own interests,
but also to the interests of others.
Your attitude should be the same as that of Christ Jesus.
PHILIPPIANS 2:4-5

Upward Gaze

To You, O God, belong the heavens, even the highest heavens, the earth and everything in it. You are mighty and awesome (Deuteronomy 10:14,17). Your name is majestic in all the earth. You've set Your glory above the heavens and ordained praise to silence the foe and the avenger (Psalm 8:1-2). Heaven is Your throne, and the earth is Your footstool (Isaiah 66:1). What a mighty God You are! Amen.

MOM

Kim and I were running errands on her eighth birthday when we passed a neighbor's driveway. Inky-feathered crows hopped around three yellow garbage sacks, ripping holes through the plastic with their beaks. Chip bags, egg cartons, a stray shoe, and squished leftovers littered the grass.

Serves her right, I gloated, noting that the woman's van wasn't in the driveway. She wasn't one of my favorite people—petty personality conflicts created static whenever our paths crossed. But then guilt poked me. *Ooooh—attitude check!* Trying to ease my conscience, I shook my head and said, "Poor lady. She'll come home to a nasty chore." *I'm glad I'm not her.*

Fifteen minutes later we passed her driveway on our way home. The crows were still partying. "If she doesn't come home soon, that mess will take forever to clean up," I said, stepping on the gas pedal. Then I heard it—a quiet voice speaking to my heart.

Pick up the trash.

Who said that? I wondered.

Pick up the trash.

There was no mistaking it. I knew exactly what to do. But what would Kim think? *Mom's flipped out this time! I'll just die if my friends see this!*

I pulled into a driveway a block from our house. "What are you doing?" asked Kim. "Why are you stopping here?"

"I think I'm supposed to pick up that garbage," I said. "You can walk home if you like. I'll be there in a few minutes." I didn't relish the thought of handling someone's used tissue or food scraps. How could I expect her to feel otherwise?

Rather than bolting from the car, she replied, "I'll help."

Kim's eager response left me speechless. I turned the car around, ashamed of my attitude. *Father, forgive me. Thanks for second chances,* I prayed silently.

Together we collected the trash and stuffed it into plastic grocery bags, then returned home to celebrate her special day.

Coincidentally, I was to speak at a women's meeting the following day. The theme of my talk? *Jesus Christ—the perfect model of humility and servanthood.* Scripture says that although He is God, He didn't consider equality with God something to be grasped. Rather, from a heart of loving compassion, He emptied himself of the glory He deserved, endured men's mocking and false accusations, and died on the cross for self-centered, grudge-bearing, proud, ungrateful people like me.

Jesus' example teaches us to do likewise. If He could die for the wayward and weak, we can live for others—even individuals we have a hard time loving. After all, we're not perfect either. Maybe others struggle to love or like us and rely on the Lord's strength to do it!

At any rate, we're surrounded with opportunities to practice humility and service. Sitting at a sick child's bedside throughout the night, providing rides for a single mom without her own vehicle, visiting the elderly in nursing homes, or cooking dinner for a family whose mother suffers chronic illness might not be convenient, but those activities can demonstrate love and practical servanthood, and God blesses them.

Inward Glimpse

Dear Father, thank You for modeling Your love through Jesus' servant attitude. Please form that same attitude in me so others will come to understand Your love for them. Amen.

- Read the hymn, "Not I, but Christ" on the next page. How can you apply these words to your own life?
- Write a short prayer to ask God to work in your life so Christ is seen in all you do.

Outward Glance

Father, I pray that _____ will be motivated to look beyond her own personal interests to the interests of others. May she display the same attitude as Christ Jesus, who emptied Himself and took on the very nature of a servant. Grant her a humble heart, one emptied of self and filled with the Holy Spirit so others will be drawn to the Savior (Philippians 2:4-8). Amen.

One More Peek

We who are strong ought to bear with the failings of the weak and not to please ourselves. Each of us should please his neighbor for his good, to build him up. For even Christ did not please himself but, as it is written: "The insults of those who insult you have fallen on me" (Romans 15:1-3).

Not I, but Christ

A.A. Whiddington

Not I, but Christ, be honored, loved, exalted;
Not I, but Christ, be seen, be known, be heard;
Not I, but Christ, in every look and action;
Not I, but Christ, in every thought and word.

Not I, but Christ, to gently soothe in sorrow;
Not I, but Christ, to wipe the falling tear;
Not I, but Christ, to lift the weary burden!
Not I, but Christ, to hush away all fear.

Not I, but Christ, in lowly, silent labor;
Not I, but Christ, in humble, earnest toil;
Christ, only Christ! to show no ostentation!
Christ, none but Christ, the gatherer of the spoil.

Oh, to be saved from myself, dear Lord,
Oh, to be lost in Thee;
Oh, that it may be no more I,
But Christ that lives in me.

Job Description

I can do everything through him who gives me strength.
PHILIPPIANS 4:13

Upward Gaze

Heavenly Father, You are the great I AM (Exodus 3:14). Through Jesus Christ You displayed Your character— Wonderful Counselor, Mighty God, everlasting Father, Prince of Peace (Isaiah 9:6). I praise You—because You are all that and more, and You will enable me to mother with excellence! Amen.

MOM

How might a mother's job description read? Try this:

Must endure nausea for several weeks or months at the job's outset. Must tolerate her body stretching to unbelievable dimensions. Must withstand excruciating pain to deliver the fruit of her labor.

After product delivery, a mother must function happily despite sleep deprivation for the next 18 years per child. Understand a crying baby's language. Answer phone calls and tend to a toddler while preparing dinner and nursing an infant. Cook economical, nutritious meals according to family members' preferences and allergies. Be present in two or more locations at once. Possess inner radar to locate children's misplaced belongings. Hold a degree in medicine and psychology. Bake countless cookies and cupcakes for school fund-raisers. Cheer budding athletes in rain or shine. Treasure sticky kisses. Keep children's baby teeth in nightstand drawer (don't ask me how I know this). Understand new math (optional). Wear extra-strong knee pads for hours spent in prayer. Forgive and request forgiveness over and over and over. *Love* unconditionally even when it's hard to *like*.

I'm just getting started! Our task's enormity overwhelms me. In all honesty, we cannot possibly do this job on our own. Certain days make me holler, "Heaven help me!" And that's exactly what happens. Someone much stronger, wiser, kinder, and smarter than I am rushes to my rescue.

And God is the perfect rescuer. When I'm confused about what makes my kids tick, the Scriptures tell me that He knit them together in my womb (Psalm 139:13). He knows why they act and react the way they do. He knows their strengths and weaknesses and what He must do to conform them to Jesus Christ's image.

When I'm weary, God reminds me that strength comes from Him— the one who created heaven and earth and holds the universe in place, the one who never slumbers nor sleeps. Through His written Word, He reminds me that when I wait on Him, He strengthens me to rise up on eagles' wings (Isaiah 40:31).

When the only person I feel sorry for is me, the Bible shows me that God is the King of compassion—He defends the oppressed (my kids are glad to know that!), gives food to the hungry, sets prisoners free (don't tell Junior that when you banish him to his room), and gives sight to the blind (Psalm 146:6-8). And His example, through the death of His Son on my behalf, teaches me that He exercises compassion even when the recipients don't deserve it.

On days when I'm tempted to complain about my task's immensity, the Word instructs me to practice thanksgiving at all times and in every situation. Why? Because that attitude reveals a solid trust in God's sovereignty and provisions in my life, a faith that He will equip me for every aspect of my job.

He'll equip you, too, dear mom. Remember—God is who He says He is. And because of that, He'll enable you to perform your task with excellence.

Inward Glimpse

Dear Father, thank You for equipping me to do this task. Help me remember I'm not doing it alone. Amen.

- What part of your job description do you enjoy most? Why?

- What part do you appreciate least? Write a prayer to God, asking Him to change your heart and grant overwhelming victory in that area.

Outward Glance

Father, I pray that _____ will recognize You as her source of wisdom and strength. May she understand that she can do all things through Christ who strengthens her (Philippians 4:13). Grant that she, according to Your glorious riches, may be strengthened with power through Your Holy Spirit in her inner being (Ephesians 3:16). Amen.

One More Peek

Praise the LORD.
How good it is to sing praises to our God,
*   how pleasant and fitting to praise him!...*
He heals the brokenhearted
*   and binds up their wounds....*
The LORD sustains the humble
*   but casts the wicked to the ground.*
Sing to the LORD with thanksgiving;
*   make music to our God on the harp....*
The LORD delights in those who fear him,
*   who put their hope in his unfailing love* (Psalm 147:1,3,6-7,11).

Little Love Notes

*And he passed in front of Moses, proclaiming, "The LORD,
the LORD, the compassionate and gracious God, slow to anger,
abounding in love and faithfulness, maintaining love to thousands,
and forgiving wickedness, rebellion and sin."*
EXODUS 34:6-7

Upward Gaze

I praise You today because Your love reaches to the heavens and Your faithfulness to the skies (Psalm 36:5). Their depth can't be measured, and they're always available to me. When my soul is downcast within me, I remember that Your compassions never fail. They're new every morning. Great is Your faithfulness! (Lamentations 3:20-23). Amen.

MOM

Gene and I met as summer camp coworkers. By summer's end, we'd grown to care deeply about each other. Gene proposed; I accepted. Then we went our separate ways—Gene returned to his family's Washington home, and I went back to Alberta to fulfill a job to which I'd committed earlier that spring.

Ours was a long-distance engagement sprinkled with monthly visits, countless letters, phone calls, and little love notes. One day after Gene had visited, a strange pill bottle in my medicine cabinet caught my attention. *That's odd,* I thought. *I don't recognize this prescription.* The label was missing, so I unscrewed the cap and peeked inside. To my delight,

I found 30 clear plastic capsules stuffed with handwritten love notes—
one for each day until we could meet again. I felt so loved, so special!

After our wedding, I tucked notes into Gene's lunches. Sometimes
I found little sentiments in my Bible. I hid messages in Gene's suitcase
when business trips called him away from home. He left notes in various locations around the house so I would find them in his absence.
When I began attending writers' conferences, he put notes in my purse
or carry-on bag.

Over the years we've done the same thing for our children. If I
accompanied Gene on a business trip, we left encouraging notes for
them to open each morning until we returned. We stashed notes in their
school lunches and in their suitcases when they left home to attend
summer camp.

The kids have left notes for us, too. One of my all-time favorite
Christmas gifts was a note from Matthew written when he was 16 years
old. Using the letters of my name, he designed an acrostic of character qualities he appreciates in my life. A "keep forever" treasure!

Have you ever considered God's Word as a collection of love notes
written especially for you? Every chapter and verse contains
reminders of His incredible love. Often they're brought to our attention at just the right time—when we're discouraged, seeking direction,
fearful, or just tired. When the household cash inflow doesn't equal the
outflow, a verse reminds us that God will provide for our needs. When
we're feeling lonely or betrayed, another verse reassures us of His presence and unconditional love. When grief strikes, Scripture brings
comfort and hope.

God's love notes appear in other forms, too. He splashes breathtaking
pink sunrises and sunsets across the sky for us to enjoy. He sends us
flowers every spring—yellow daffodils, purple hyacinths, and red prim-
roses—and a rainbow after storms. He sends the sparrows as visual
reminders that He's mindful of our needs and will provide for us just
as He does for them. He embraces us through a child's sticky kiss or
enthusiastic hug.

And just as He lavishes His love on us through special encourage-
ments, we can do the same for our friends and families. A greeting card

tells someone we're thinking of him or her. A love note taped to the steering wheel of our husband's car, on our daughter's mirror, or our son's baseball glove reassures them of our love. A note left on our children's pillow, commending a thoughtful deed or positive character quality, makes them feel embraced.

Where's God's love note for you today? Keep your eyes open!

Inward Glimpse

Dear God, help me to find the love notes You leave for me each day. And help me to pass Your love along to other people. Amen.

- How has God shown His love to you in the past week?
- Write a love note for each member of your family. Tuck them in special places.

Outward Glance

Heavenly Father, just as You're faithful to us each day, I ask that _____ will be faithful to You. May he love and serve you with all his heart and soul (Deuteronomy 11:13). I pray that he will sing of Your love forever and make known Your faithfulness throughout all generations. May he know and declare that Your love stands firm forever. May his life declare that You established Your faithfulness in heaven itself (Psalm 89:1-2). Amen.

One More Peek

Your love, O LORD, reaches to the heavens,
your faithfulness to the skies.
Your righteousness is like the mighty mountains,
your justice like the great deep.

O Lord, you preserve both man and beast.
   How priceless is your unfailing love!
Both high and low among men
   find refuge in the shadow of your wings.
They feast on the abundance of your house;
   you give them drink from your river of delights.
For with you is the fountain of life;
   in your light we see light (Psalm 36:5-9).

Engraved on His Palms

See, I have engraved you on the palm of my hands;
your walls are ever before me.
ISAIAH 49:16

Upward Gaze

Father, You are worthy of praise because You are all-knowing. You give wisdom to the wise and knowledge to the discerning. You reveal deep and hidden things; You know what lies in darkness, and light dwells with You (Daniel 2:21-22). You are great and mighty in power. I praise You, for Your understanding has no limit (Psalm 147:5). Amen.

MOM

Hands are useful for a myriad of activities—playing musical instruments, applying makeup, washing dishes, braiding hair, waving goodbye. They're also handy for helping their owners remember important facts...until soap hits them, that is.

That happened to me (again) after a bright pink poster grabbed my attention. Local Craft Fair! Reserve Your Table Now! It listed all the important information: date, location, time, and organizer's phone number.

That sounds like fun! I thought. *Selling homemade crafts—a good way to earn extra Christmas cash.*

I rummaged through my purse for a paper scrap, a gum wrapper, a tissue, anything on which to write the phone number, but I came up empty. The next best thing was obvious—my hand. I scribbled the number on my palm and double-checked for accuracy.

I should have transferred the information to a piece of paper immediately upon arriving at home, but as usual, busyness abounded. The phone rang, the kids clamored for my attention, the cat meowed for dinner, and the washing machine ker-thumped its way across the utility room floor.

Two hours later, after cooking dinner and washing dishes, I plopped onto the couch beside Gene. "Today I saw a poster about a craft fair," I said. "I'll reserve my table this evening."

I reached for the phone and glanced at my palm for the number. To my dismay, the digits were gone. They'd disappeared down the drain with the dirty dishwater.

Scripture says God writes on His palms, too, but His method far supersedes mine. Two thousand years ago, His Son received a death sentence for a crime He didn't commit. He hung on a splintery wooden cross from rough nails that soldiers pounded through His hands and feet.

For Christ, those nail prints signified sacrificial death. For men and women who place their saving faith in Him, they signify new life. Unlike ink, those nail prints can't be washed away. They're forever visible, constant reminders of the men and women for whom He died.

"Can a mother forget the baby at her breast and have no compassion on the child she has borne? Though she may forget, I will not forget you!" God says to His people. "See, I have engraved you on the palms of my hands; your walls are ever before me" (Isaiah 49:15-16).

Regardless of the promise, we face days when we feel as though God has forgotten us. We feel lonely, left out, unwanted, and unimportant. Perhaps a coworker's comments hurt us. The car breaks down, the dishwasher dies, the washing machine quits, and the kids catch the flu. We wonder if somehow our name has been erased from God's memory.

Be encouraged, dear moms! Every moment of every day, we're on His mind. Even while we're asleep, He's thinking about us, watching over us, guiding and guarding us. Such knowledge brings courage and confidence to face whatever a day brings.

The next time we feel as though God has forgotten us, we can remember the nail prints in Christ's hands. Nothing can wash His scars away. His hands bear a constant reminder of His great love.

Inward Glimpse

Father, thank You for engraving me on the palms of Your hands. Help me remember that You can't forget me. Amen.

- Read the hymn, "Moment by Moment" on the next page. Which stanza means the most to you, and why?
- Memorize today's key verse.

Outward Glance

Dear Father, I pray that _____ will never forget Your name or spread out her hands to a foreign god (Psalm 44:20). When her spirit grows faint, remind her that You know her way (Psalm 142:3). Remind her that You, the omniscient God, not only know her name but also know the number of hairs on her head (Matthew 10:30). Amen.

One More Peek

How precious to me are your thoughts, O God!
  How vast is the sum of them!
Were I to count them,
  they would outnumber the grains of sand.
When I awake,
  I am still with you (Psalm 139:17-18).

Moment by Moment

Daniel W. Whittle

Dying with Jesus, by death reckoned mine:
Living with Jesus, a new life divine;
Looking to Jesus till glory doth shine,
Moment by moment, O Lord, I am Thine.

Never a trial that He is not there,
Never a burden that He doth not bear,
Never a sorrow that He doth not share,
Moment by moment, I'm under His care.

Never a heartache and never a groan,
Never a teardrop and never a moan;
Never a danger, but there on the throne,
Moment by moment, He thinks of His own.

Moment by moment I'm kept in His love;
Moment by moment I've life from above;
Looking to Jesus till glory doth shine;
Moment by moment, O Lord, I am Thine.

I Want to Go Fast!

Be still before the LORD and wait patiently for him.
PSALM 37:7

Upward Gaze

Heavenly Father, I praise You because You are a God of compassion and justice, and You bless all who wait for You (Isaiah 30:18). No ear has heard or eye has seen any God like You, who acts on behalf of those who wait for You (Isaiah 64:4). You are my portion. I will wait for You (Lamentations 3:24). Amen.

Sunshine warmed Vikki's back as she unloaded four-year-old Jordan's bike from her car's trunk. "This park is perfect for riding your bike," she said to her son. "You can pedal on and on and on!"

"Goodie!" Jordan exclaimed, clapping his hands. "Can I ride over there?" he asked, pointing at a nearby sidewalk.

"Sure!" Vikki answered. "But I want you to stay near me, okay?"

"Okay," Jordan agreed. Vikki helped him adjust his helmet, and the twosome began their afternoon adventure. For a while, Jordan kept his word. But as his confidence grew, he pedaled faster. The span widened between his mom and him. He pedaled still faster.

"Stop, Jordan!" called Vikki when she realized the situation. Her command went unheeded. The preschooler's legs only worked harder. "Stop!" she yelled again. Still no response. Feeling uncomfortable with the growing distance between her and her son, she ran to catch up.

Seconds later Vikki pulled the bike to a halt. She knelt and looked in Jordan's eyes. "I told you to stop. Didn't you hear me?"

"Sure, Mom, but I was going as fast as a jet plane," he answered.

"But you didn't listen to me," she said.

"I wanted to go fast," he countered.

I wanted to go fast. I've said those words a few times—to God. How many times have I rushed ahead of Him?

I want you to stay near me, He says. *I want you to take a sabbatical of sorts—a quiet season of learning to listen to My voice.*

"Okay," I agree. I'm fine with that…until dawdling wearies me. One day the phone rings. "The women's ministry needs a new chairperson. Would you take the position?"

"It would be a privilege!" I pedal faster.

The phone rings again. "Would you be willing to teach the two- and three-year-olds' Sunday school class?"

"I'd love to!" My legs work harder.

The phone rings once more. This time it's my boss. "You've done a magnificent job at work. We'd like to give you a new position—more hours, more pay. What do you say?"

"Wow—sounds great!" The distance widens between God and me. In my pursuit of wonderful opportunities, I overlook God's caution, "I want you to stay near Me, okay?" Somewhere back there I hear a faint, *Stop, Grace!* but I can't be sure. I just want to go fast.

Abraham felt that way, too. Scripture says God promised that his descendants would be too numerous to count. He told Abraham to wait and watch for the promise's fulfillment.

What did the man do? He pedaled faster. *My wife and I are getting too old for this,* he thought. *I'll speed up whatever God is trying to do.* Rather than enjoying his journey beside God, he forged ahead and fathered a child by his wife's maid. His disobedience carried consequences.

Jordan's disobedience carried consequences, too. He lost his freedom. Vikki insisted that he ride beside her all the way back to the car.

Like Abraham and Jordan, our rushing ahead also carries consequences. Failing to stop could result in a spill—our health collapses, our marriage falters, our kids get into trouble. We could take the wrong path and ride into a bad situation.

God's plans for us are good, but we need to work within His time frame. He wants to protect us. He wants to fellowship with us along the journey.

Inward Glimpse

Heavenly Father, thank You for wanting me to stay near You. Help me not to rush ahead of Your plans. Amen.

- Recall an instance when you rushed ahead of God. What happened?
- If you're struggling with waiting on God for something specific right now, what is it? Write a prayer in which you ask God to help you be patient.

Outward Glance

Father, I pray that _____ will confidently wait on You and see Your goodness. Make her resolve strong as she waits on You, her help and shield. May her heart rejoice in You, trusting in Your holy name (Psalm 27:14; 33:20-21). Amen.

One More Peek

The LORD had said to Abram, "Leave your country, your people and your father's household and go to the land I will show you.

"I will make you into a great nation
and I will bless you;
I will make your name great,
and you will be a blessing.
I will bless those who bless you,
and whoever curses you I will curse;
and all peoples on earth
will be blessed through you" (Genesis 12:1-3).

Daddy Can Fix It

The LORD is good,
a refuge in times of trouble.
He cares for those who trust in him.
NAHUM 1:7

Upward Gaze

Sovereign LORD, You've made the heavens and earth by Your great power and outstretched arm. Nothing is too hard for You (Jeremiah 32:17). I praise You for being a refuge to those who trust in You (Psalm 62:8). I praise You for being my fortress in times of trouble and for showing me loving-kindness (Psalm 59:16-17). Amen.

MOM

My next-door neighbor's sons, Bradley and Joel, own homemade rubber band guns. Each gun required a wooden dowel, a clothespin, and a piece of wood shaped like a revolver. Their dad carefully glued the three parts together. After the glue dried, the boys stretched rubber bands into place, took aim at the nearest rock, and let 'er rip.

"Hey, I have an idea!" said Bradley after a few minutes. "Let's shoot tin cans!"

"Yeah, let's!" Joel agreed. They set up their targets and aimed again. Before Bradley pressed the clothespin trigger, however, his gun's dowel fell off. A minute later, Joel's did the same thing.

"Oh, no!" Joel exclaimed. "This isn't supposed to happen!" The boys ran to their mom and showed her the loose parts.

"That's not a problem," she reassured them. "Perhaps the glue wasn't dry enough. Daddy can fix them when he comes home." Sure enough, their dad glued the parts together again. This time they waited a couple of days. Their fun lasted for several weeks until the toys had been dropped once too often on the concrete sidewalk outside their house.

"What's wrong with these things?" asked Joel, looking at the loose pieces in his hand.

"Broken again," sighed Bradley. Then he added confidently, "Oh well. Daddy can fix them."

Another friend's three-year-old child displayed the same faith in his dad, a surgeon, when we camped with his family in Alaska. One afternoon, Gene discovered the little daredevil walking on the motor home's roof.

"Come down," Gene said. "You'll hurt yourself if you fall off."

"That's okay," replied the boy. "My daddy's a doctor. He stitches me up. He always fixes me."

Wouldn't you enjoy a faith in God as simple and confident as the boys' trust in their fathers? Too often, though, we want to know *how* God is going to fix something before we're convinced He's capable.

I can believe God can accomplish anything if I understand how He'll do it. But when apparent impossibility wipes out possibility, my faith falters. I need to remember that when God chooses to act, nothing stops His power. His authority moves beyond the realm of the rational and reasonable.

My desire is to unconditionally trust God just as Joel and Bradley and the adventuresome three-year-old trusted their dads without question. I pray this is your desire, too. Together our faith will grow as God's character guides our thoughts and our actions every day.

As that happens, our outlooks will change. Our kids and others around us will see confidence in us. Not confidence that life will always be problem free, but assurance that God will fix the hurts. He may not always do it the way we want or in our timing, but He'll always do it to glorify and draw people to Himself.

Inward Glimpse

Father, thank You for fixing my hurts. Help me trust You even when the situation looks impossible. Amen.

- What circumstances seem impossible to you today?
- Write a prayer to acknowledge God's ability to meet you there.

Outward Glance

Father, I pray that _____ will trust in You for his deliverance from trials and testings. Answer him when he cries out to You. Please don't disappoint him when he places his trust in You (Psalm 22:4-5). Amen.

One More Peek

I am the resurrection and the life. He who believes in me will live, even though he dies; and whoever lives and believes in me will never die (John 11:25-26).

Awesome God

How awesome is the LORD Most High,
the great King over all the earth.
PSALM 47:2

Upward Gaze

Father, I praise You because You are majestic in holiness, awesome in glory, a worker of wonders (Exodus 15:11). You are the God of gods and the Lord of lords, the great God, mighty and awesome (Deuteronomy 10:17). Amen.

MOM

Donna glanced at the dashboard clock as she drove up her driveway. *It's 11:30. I'll unload groceries and fix lunch. After that I'll sip hot tea and sew—a pleasant way to spend a wintry afternoon!*

She reached for the keys, but before she could turn off the ignition, her heart began pounding inside her chest. Goose bumps covered her arms.

What's wrong? she thought. *Something's very wrong!* Panic seized her as images of her 16-year-old son, Darrell, flashed through her mind. *Where is he? Is he in danger?* The prospect terrified her.

Suddenly a still, small voice nudged, *Pray!*

Without a moment's hesitation, Donna obeyed. "God, something's wrong somewhere! Someone needs help. Perhaps it's Darrell. You know exactly where he is. You know his needs. Please send Your angels to protect him. Keep him from harm. Surround him, save him, defeat the enemy who seeks to destroy him." She paused for a moment and then prayed again, repeating her pleas for God's protection and praising Him for His ability to answer.

After several minutes, the sense of urgency passed. She closed her prayer with an "Amen" and set about unloading her groceries. Many times throughout the afternoon, her thoughts returned to Darrell.

She heard his truck's familiar rumble as darkness fell. Two doors slammed, and he and a friend stepped into the house. "Hey, Mom! We're home," he called as she hustled down the hall and into the kitchen.

"I'm glad for that!" she exclaimed. "How was your day? Anything unusual happen?"

"Yeah, you wouldn't believe it," Darrell answered. His buddy nodded in agreement.

"Try me," said Donna.

"We were driving on a highway that was an icy mess," he said. "The truck slid into the ditch and started to roll, but all of a sudden we were back on the road. Go figure."

Donna raised her eyebrows. "What time did that happen?"

"Eleven-thirty."

Donna smiled and told her side of the story to the two astonished teens. She recalled the situation as she prepared for bed later that evening. *What an awesome God! When He knew the boys were in trouble, His Holy Spirit prompted me to pray, and He protected them from danger at that exact moment!*

Donna's experience reinforces a truth that Scripture declares over and over—God is awesome. And because He is awesome in character, He performs awesome deeds.

Scripture tells the story of the Israelites' exodus from Egypt. Indeed, it's one incredible account! After plaguing the Egyptians with one problem after another, God split the Red Sea so the Israelites could cross on dry land and then drowned the Egyptian army behind them. He used Moses to lead the people with a cloud during the daytime and a pillar of fire by night. He fed and watered their millions every day for 40 years. He kept their clothes and sandals from wearing out.

Why did He do that? Besides fulfilling His eternal plan, perhaps He had another reason. Deuteronomy 4:34-35 says that He performed these awesome deeds "so that you might know that the LORD is God; besides him there is no other." God wanted to get the Israelites' attention. He wanted them to acknowledge Him as the one and only God because He loved them and desired unbroken fellowship with His people.

God still performs awesome deeds. A fetus' development and birth, a child's vivid imagination, autumn leaves' changing array, the star-spattered heavens, miraculous answers to prayer—they all exemplify His mighty power.

Dear mom, my prayer for you today is that you might see His awesome deeds all around you and that as you do, you will know and understand Him as a truly awesome God.

Inward Glimpse

Dear Father, thank You for performing awesome deeds. Help me be faithful to You, the one and only awesome God. Amen.

- What awesome deeds have you witnessed?
- Teach your children today's key verse. Ask them what they think *awesome* means when referring to God. Write their remarks.

Outward Glance

Heavenly Father, I pray that _____ will see Your great and awesome wonders with her own eyes. And when she does, may she recognize You as her praise and her God (Deuteronomy 10:21). May she declare You as an awesome God, the God who gives strength and power to His people (Psalm 68:35). Amen.

One More Peek

Say to God, "How awesome are your deeds!
So great is your power

that your enemies cringe before you.
All the earth bows down to you;
   they sing praise to you,
   they sing praise to your name." Selah
Come and see what God has done,
   how awesome his works in man's behalf!
   (Psalm 66:3-5).

His Majesty

Who among the gods is like you, O LORD?
Who is like you—majestic in holiness,
awesome in glory, working wonders?
EXODUS 15:11

Upward Gaze

I will exalt You, my God the King; I will praise Your name for ever and ever (Psalm 145:1). You are great and worthy of praise—no one can fully fathom the extent of Your greatness. Generations will speak of Your mighty acts and tell of the glorious splendor of Your majesty (Psalm 145:3-5). Your kingdom is everlasting, and Your dominion endures through all generations (Psalm 145:13). You are my King! You are my Lord! I love You and praise Your name. Amen.

Scripture says God is majestic. What exactly does that mean? According to J.I. Packer in his book *Knowing God*, our word *majesty* comes from a Latin word that means "greatness." Packer writes, "When we ascribe majesty to someone, we are acknowledging greatness in that person, and voicing our respect for it: as, for instance, when we speak of 'Her Majesty' the Queen."[6]

Imagine, for a moment, the pomp and pageantry that accompanies royal celebrations. When England's late Queen Mother celebrated her one hundredth birthday in July, 2000, London staged the largest parade in that country's history. Bands played and military armies fired salutes as the dignified birthday girl smiled and waved to her cheering fans outside Buckingham Palace. Prancing horses pulled her royal carriage through streets lined with thousands of adoring subjects. For the first time in public, her daughter, Queen Elizabeth, walked behind her to signify honor and preference.

Why did the crowds hold the Queen Mother in such high regard? The answer is twofold. First, her position commanded respect. While her husband was king, she wore the title of Her Majesty the Queen. The birthday celebration acknowledged the position she once held.

Second, her personal behavior warranted respect. Throughout her reign, she exemplified dignity and displayed love for others. People trusted her. They considered her to be a woman of greatness. When she made personal appearances, people lined the streets, hoping for the opportunity to greet her personally or give her fresh flowers.

The Queen Mother was merely human but received royal treatment. If she commanded such a high degree of respect and honor, imagine how much more God, the heavenly Father, deserves!

God's position warrants our worship. He's the Creator and King of the universe. He's the blessed controller of all things and giver of eternal life. He's the one true God!

His behavior leads us to honor him. He's sinless—He has never done nor can do wrong. He's filled with love for His subjects. He proved His love by sending Jesus Christ to die on the cross to suffer the consequences for our sin and purchase eternal life for us. He answers prayer, promises to be with us in every circumstance, and gives victory over sin. And that's just the beginning!

How should we respond to "His Majesty"? We can hold Him in high regard and recognize His greatness. When we read the Bible, we can choose to obey its words, knowing that God authored them, and His authority is stamped all over them. And we can model our lives after Jesus because He demonstrated His Father's nature—kind, patient, loving, without sin.

Inward Glimpse

Heavenly Father, You are the Creator, our sustainer and guide. Help me to honor You in all I say and do.

- What does God's greatness mean to you?
- Meditate on the words of the hymn "Majestic Sweetness Sits Enthroned" on the next page. Memorize a verse and recall it when you have a few minutes to yourself.

Outward Glance

Almighty King, open _____'s spiritual eyes to see and understand Your majesty. Help him understand that You sit enthroned above the earth. Help him comprehend that You stretch out the heavens like a canopy, that You rule over the rulers. May he lift his eyes and look to the heavens, recognizing that You created all the starry host and call each one by name (Isaiah 40:22-26). May he acknowledge You as Lord, the everlasting God (Isaiah 40:28).

One More Peek

I know that you can do all things;
no plan of yours can be thwarted....
Surely I spoke of things I did not understand,
things too wonderful for me to know....
My ears had heard of you
but now my eyes have seen you (Job 42:2-3,5).

Majestic Sweetness
Sits Enthroned

Samuel Stennett

Majestic sweetness sits enthroned upon the Savior's brow;
His head with radiant glories crowned, His lips with grace o'erflow,
His lips with grace o'erflow.

No mortal can with Him compare, among the sons of men;
Fairer is He than all the fair that fill the heavenly train,
That fill the heavenly train.

He saw me plunged in deep distress, He flew to my relief;
For me He bore the shameful cross and carried all my grief,
And carried all my grief.

To Him I owe my life and breath, and all the joys I have;
He makes me triumph over death, and saves me from the grave,
And saves me from the grave.

Since from His bounty I receive such proofs of love divine,
Had I a thousand hearts to give, Lord, they should all be Thine,
Lord, they should all be Thine.

Good Enough?

But God demonstrates his own love for us in this:
While we were still sinners, Christ died for us.
ROMANS 5:8

Upward Gaze

Father, You are perfect in every way (Matthew 5:48). You don't change like shifting shadows (James 1:17). Yet, in Your holy perfection, You reached to me through Your Son. I praise You for sending Jesus to die for me even though I was ungodly and undeserving (Romans 5:6). Amen.

— MOM —

Vikki kissed four-year-old Jordan goodnight and quietly closed the bedroom door behind her. Moments later, she opened her journal and penned the following: *Today was a rough day. Jordan repeatedly tested his boundaries, and I disciplined him several times. Finally he said, "I'm no good. I'm not good enough for you. Why don't you find another son?"*

Vikki's heart ached as she read and reread the words, recalling Jordan's outbursts. She mentally processed her son's words for several days, and as she did, a realization dawned. *That's exactly how I feel sometimes— no good. When I fail and sin, I'm tempted to say, "I'm not good enough to be your daughter, God. Find someone else to do what You need done."*

Vikki isn't the only mom who has struggled with these thoughts. I have, too. In fact, my fear of not measuring up stems back to fourth grade. I remember my schoolteacher walking between the rows of desks, passing out graded math exams.

I'm no good at math, I convinced myself as she approached my desk. *I probably failed.* I cringed, imagining a big red "F." My stomach formed knots. They grew tighter and tighter until I thrust my hand up and blurted a lie. "I think I'm going to throw up!"

"Oh dear," said the teacher. "You'd better run to the washroom."

No good, no good, no good echoed through my mind as I charged down the hall. I hid in a stall until the teacher came in.

"I've asked the principal to drive you home," she said. That wasn't what I'd expected. By the time I got home, Mom had been notified of the suspected flu bug. She kept me in bed for two days. Upon my return to school, my teacher returned the graded test.

I passed the math exam but failed the life lesson.

Negative thoughts continued throughout high school and college. My self-worth hit rock bottom after a brief engagement ended. I compared myself to other young women—their physical appearance, friendships, and talents—and convinced myself that I was indeed inferior.

Several months after graduation, I attended a women's conference with the theme "You Are Very Special." The speaker's biblical messages stressed that God loves people because He is love, not because we earn His love or deserve it. In fact, if His love for us was based upon whether or not we met His standard of holiness, we would be out of luck! His love is a gift, not a reward for human perfection.

That fact liberated me! I gradually overcame the fear of failure, the incessant nagging to perform flawlessly. Occasionally, I still hear the old echo—*no good, no good.* But when I do, I refuse to entertain it. Instead, I counteract it with memorized Scripture or praise. And if I slip into comparing myself with other women and grow discouraged with the results, I remind myself that God loves me as I am.

God treasures us. He values us. He doesn't want to go out and find other daughters to take our places. He wants *us.*

Inward Glimpse

Dear Father, thank You for loving me as I am. Help me reflect Your unconditional love to other people. Amen.

- In what areas of your life do you feel you're not good enough? Write a prayer of thanks to God for not expecting perfection. Ask Him to remove the nagging sense of not measuring up.
- According to Exodus 3–4, how did Moses feel when God called him to lead the Israelites? How did God respond?

Outward Glance

Heavenly Father, please help _____ understand that perfection doesn't earn Your favor; You love her simply because You are love. Help her understand what You require of her—to act justly and love mercy and to walk humbly with You (Micah 6:8)—and give her a desire to pursue that as her goal. Amen.

One More Peek

Who gave man his mouth? Who makes him deaf or mute? Who gives him sight or makes him blind? Is it not I, the LORD? Now go; I will help you speak and will teach you what to say (Exodus 4:11-12).

Look at My Eyes!

You rule over the surging sea;
when its waves mount up, you still them.
PSALM 89:9

Upward Gaze

I will sing of Your love forever, LORD. I'll talk about Your faithfulness to young and old. Your love stands firm forever. Your faithfulness has been established in heaven itself (Psalm 89:1-2). No one is like You! You are mighty, surrounded by Your faithfulness (Psalm 89:8). When we cry out, You answer with awesome deeds of righteousness. You formed the mountains by Your power and still the roaring of the waves (Psalm 65:5-7). You are worthy to be trusted. Amen.

◄ MOM ►

Saturday dawned with grey sky and drizzle, but that wouldn't stop us! No, sir. Layers of clothing topped with yellow raingear promised to keep us warm and dry. We would sail around Quadra Island, come what may. A little liquid sunshine wouldn't dampen our enthusiasm.

Eight hours into our adventure, the morning breeze blew stronger. Before long, a howling wind surrounded us—every purebred sailor's dream come true. The 25-foot boat heeled far to port as it bounced and sliced its way through white-capped waves. A half-dozen college-age passengers clung to the lines as they stretched backward over the water, shrieking with excitement.

I clung and shrieked, too. Silently. I don't even like cold showers. The thought of dumping into frigid saltwater waves terrorized me. Lorne, our boat's skipper, grinned. "Now you can say you've sailed in gale force winds!"

"Whoopee!" I answered, hoping to mask my fear. *And people think this is fun?* Suddenly, screams from the boat's cabin shattered my thoughts.

"Help! I'm gonna drown," 11-year-old Kim cried. "I hate this! Stop the boat!" I half-stepped, half-tumbled into the cabin to find Kim cowering in a corner. Lorne's 11-year-old daughter was attempting to console her.

"Don't be scared, Kim. This boat has never sunk. My brother was knocked overboard once, but my mom grabbed him as he floated by." Kim's eyes grew wider. "Don't worry. Everything will be okay."

The boat heeled far to starboard, this time pushing the windows underwater. From our cabin seats, we watched green water and air bubbles swish and swirl by. "I feel like I'm in an aquarium!" Kim shrieked. Her visible terror reflected my thoughts exactly, but I couldn't help her if I screamed, too.

Mentally I trusted the skipper's skill and the boat's capabilities, but my emotions cried the opposite. How could I tell Kim not to be afraid when I felt the same way? Suddenly an idea came to mind.

"Look at my eyes," I commanded. "Don't look out the window. Forget the water. Just look at my eyes." *And don't see the fear in them!* I added under my breath. Kim obeyed. For both her benefit and mine, I prayed, "God, You're more powerful than the storm. You can calm it with a simple word. Keep us safe. Thanks for being with us right now." The wind blew, the boat tossed, but the panic eased.

Sometimes the winds of change blow into our lives. A job promotion means transferring to a new office, uprooting the kids, making new friends, finding a suitable house. Perhaps a close friend moves away or a spouse decides to toss aside his marriage vows. Waves of fear crash around us. A phone call brings tragic news or a teenager runs away from home. Uncertainty swirls around us, threatening to dump us from security into the dark unknown.

Jesus knows all about storms. Accused of a crime He didn't commit, He bore floggings and death on a cross. In the midst of it, He cried to God, "Why have You forsaken me?" He understands our questions and pain when life's waves and whitecaps batter us.

Like a loving parent, He stays beside us during those difficult times. "Look at Me," He says. "Pay no attention to the storm. It won't hurt you. It will soon be over. Just look at Me." His eyes reflect compassion, joy, love, and peace. And just as His resurrection defeated death, He promises victory to us when the storm passes.

When we experience that peace, people around us will notice a difference in our lives. Like a safe harbor, our relationship with Jesus will draw them so they might find Him to be their refuge, too.

Inward Glimpse

Dear God, thank You for being Master of the wind and waves. Help me focus on You when storms blow. Fill my heart with the peace and joy that come from knowing Jesus. I ask this in His name. Amen.

- What storms are you facing today? Write a short prayer to God. Ask Him to keep your focus on Him, the one who stills all storms.

- Meditate on the words of the song "Jesus, I Am Resting, Resting" on page 198.

Outward Glance

Father God, I pray that _____ will fix his eyes on Jesus Christ, the author and perfecter of faith. May he focus on Jesus rather than on discouraging or frightening circumstances in his life. May he throw off all hindrances to spiritual growth and be cleansed of the sins that would entangle him (Hebrews 12:1-2). Amen.

One More Peek

Then they cried out to the LORD in their trouble,
and he brought them out of their distress.
He stilled the storm to a whisper;
the waves of the sea were hushed.
They were glad when it grew calm,
and he guided them to their desired haven.
Let them give thanks to the LORD for his unfailing love
and his wonderful deeds for men (Psalm 107:28-31)

Jesus, I Am Resting, Resting

Jean S. Pigott

Jesus, I am resting, resting in the joy of what Thou art;
I am finding out the greatness of Thy loving heart.
Thou hast bid me gaze upon Thee, and Thy beauty fills my soul,
For by Thy transforming power, Thou hast made me whole.

Oh, how great Thy loving-kindness, vaster, broader than the sea!
Oh, how marvellous Thy goodness, lavished all on me!
Yes, I rest in Thee, Beloved, know what wealth of grace is Thine,
Know Thy certainty of promise, and have made it mine.

Simply trusting Thee, Lord Jesus, I behold Thee as Thou art,
And Thy love, so pure, so changeless, satisfies my heart;
Satisfies its deepest longings, meets, supplies its every need,
Compasseth me round with blessings: Thine is love indeed!

Ever lift Thy face upon me, as I work and wait for Thee;
Resting 'neath Thy smile, Lord Jesus, earth's dark shadows flee.
Brightness of my Father's glory, sunshine of my Father's face,
Keep me ever trusting, resting, fill me with Thy grace.

Use the Spotlight

You are my lamp, O LORD;
the LORD turns my darkness into light.
2 SAMUEL 22:29

Upward Gaze

Father, I praise You because You are light, and in You there is no darkness at all (1 John 1:5). Through Jesus Christ, Your light shines into the world, dispels darkness, and gives us the light of life (John 8:12). With You as my light and my salvation, I shall fear no one (Psalm 27:1). Amen.

Darkness spread its star-studded cape across the sky as we turned our little sailboat into Gowlland Harbor. We'd enjoyed a delightful visit onboard with friends while watching Alaskan cruise ships glide through the Inside Passage. Together we'd serenaded the sunset with oohs and aahs as God splashed pinks and golds across the sky.

But now the darkness presented a challenge. Little islands dot our local waters like sprinkles on a birthday cake. Experienced sailors maintain a healthy respect for these islands. They keep their boats a safe distance from them, knowing that jagged rocky reefs lie under the water's surface.

High tides easily cover reefs, allowing for safe travel. As the tide drops, many of these rocks are exposed. Some, however, still hide mere inches beneath the water's surface. A skipper must be alert at all times but especially at night lest he run the boat into hidden rocks and rip a hole in the vessel's hull.

Gene wasn't about to take chances. "Take the tiller, Matthew," he instructed. "We'll use the spotlight."

Matt reached for the tiller. He studied the shore's dark outlines and steered the boat down the center of the passage as Gene rummaged through the storage locker. "Here it is," he said, pulling out the handheld light. "Just what we need."

Gene carried the light to the boat's bow and flicked the switch. A light beam equal to a million candles' glow instantly lit our route. Gene scanned the water and surrounding islands with the spotlight. Each time he saw a potential danger, he positioned the beam directly on it. Using the light as his guide, Matt steered the sailboat safely back to the dock.

Sometimes our circumstances surround us like a black night. A teenage daughter confides, "I'm pregnant." The doctor delivers a diagnosis: cancer. The boss apologizes for cutbacks and hands us a pink slip. We can't see our way; we're fearful and unsure of how to respond.

But God's presence in our lives is like that spotlight. It slices through the darkness and calms our fears. He lights our path and directs us out of danger's way when we cry to Him.

Sometimes God uses His written Word to guide us. His directives and promises guard us from shipwreck if we obey them. Attempting to live without His guidance is like navigating through a rock-riddled harbor at night without proper equipment, hoping to dodge the dangers. God gives us a choice.

Shipwreck would have been certain if Matthew had chosen to say, "Thanks, but no thanks, Dad. I don't need the light. I can do this on my own." Doing so would have been foolish, just like navigating through life while ignoring God, the true Light of the world. By following the light, however, Matt maneuvered the boat through potential danger and docked safely.

And so it is with our lives. We can choose wisely, walking in the light of God's presence through a personal relationship with Jesus Christ, the Light of the world. By doing so, we'll avoid the dangers of sin and self-reliance.

Inward Glimpse

Dear Father, thank You for the light You've provided through Jesus Christ and Your written Word. Help me to walk in that light, and as I do, to show others the way. Amen.

- Have you invited Jesus, the Light of the world, to guide you through life? If the answer is yes, write a short prayer of thanks for the light of His presence in your life. If the answer is no, you can invite Him to do so now.
- God loves you more than words can say. Thank Him for His wonderful, unconditional love for you.

Outward Glance

Father of light, You've said that those who walk in the light of Your presence are blessed. I pray that would be true of _____. May she exult in Your righteousness and rejoice in Your name all day long (Psalm 89:15-16). I pray that she will live as a child of light, finding out what pleases You. May she have nothing to do with deeds of darkness but have courage to expose them (Ephesians 5:8-11). Amen.

One More Peek

There will be no more night. They will not need the light of a lamp or the light of the sun, for the Lord God will give them light. And they will reign for ever and ever (Revelation 22:5).

Watch Your Diet

Like newborn babies, crave pure spiritual milk,
so that by it you may grow up in your salvation,
now that you have tasted that the Lord is good.
1 PETER 2:2-3

Upward Gaze

Father, You're worthy of praise. In Your mercy and compassion, You've provided me with the bread of life through Jesus Christ, Your Son (John 6:35). I praise You for loving me enough to send Him to take the punishment for my sin. Amen.

MOM

Nutrition—we hear a lot about it these days. Health experts recommend that we eliminate refined flours and sugar, limit fat intake, and toss out chemically laden processed foods and hydrogenated oils. They tell us to eat raw fruits and vegetables, whole grains, natural sweeteners such as fruit juice or honey, and cold-pressed oils such as olive oil. And drink at least eight glasses of water every day.

Without a doubt, proper eating habits affect our physical and emotional well-being. Continually stuffing ourselves with pop, pizza, and potato chips produces "excess waist," which in turn affects how we feel about ourselves. Dr. Gary Smalley, author of *The Amazing Connection Between Food and Love,* explained how poor food choices can affect brain chemicals, which in turn causes specific emotional changes.

"When we're moody or grouchy or depressed or sleepy or whatever, our relationships and eventually our physical health are affected," he said. "When we don't feel lovable, it's difficult to allow others to love us or express love to them. We tend to isolate ourselves, leaving relationships weak and ourselves feeling lonely."[7]

Physical nutrition and spiritual nourishment are amazingly similar. In the physical realm, junk food tingles our tastebuds but lends nothing to our health benefits, while proper nutrition builds robust bodies and relationships. Likewise, nibbling on junk food for the soul such as steamy romance novels, sizzling soap operas, and sensuous song lyrics only builds toxic waste, which in turn weakens our relationship with the Lord and eventually affects our ties with others.

The opposite is true when we feed on God's Word. Spiritual stamina increases, positively affecting our relationship with the Lord and those around us.

Eating properly is also essential because our example easily influences our children. Seeing us feasting on God's written Word is good for them. They need to hear us praise and pray to our heavenly Father.

We can supplement our kids' spiritual intake by taking them to Sunday school regularly. We can surprise them with popular Christian music CDs for special occasions or no reason at all. We can purchase age-appropriate Christian magazine subscriptions. We can cultivate family prayer times, read Bible stories at bedtime, direct teens to well-written Christian biographies, and make ourselves available to discuss hot topics from a biblical perspective. We can open our homes to missionaries on furlough.

But most important, we can pray that our kids will come to know Jesus, the Bread of Life, as their personal Savior and find their needs met in Him.

As we watch our diet by removing spiritual junk food from the pantry of our hearts and filling up on what's best for us—God's Word, fellowship with other believers, worship, prayer—our example will model what's right for our kids. And we can trust God to work in their hearts as we pray that they'll partake, too.

Inward Glimpse

Dear Father, thank You for feeding me with Your Word. Create in me a hunger and thirst for truth and strength to resist unhealthy morsels. Amen.

- What junk food should be tossed from your spiritual pantry?
- According to today's passage in "One More Peek," in whom do we find our spiritual needs met? What does He offer?

Outward Glance

Heavenly Father, I pray that _____ will hunger and thirst for righteousness (Matthew 5:6). May she treasure the words of Your mouth more than her daily bread (Job 23:12). May she fill her spiritual diet with whatever is true, noble, right, pure, lovely, admirable, full of excellence, and praiseworthy (Philippians 4:8). Amen.

One More Peek

I am the bread of life. Your forefathers ate the manna in the desert, yet they died. But here is the bread that comes down from heaven, which a man may eat and not die. I am the living bread that came down from heaven. If anyone eats of this bread, he will live forever. This bread is my flesh, which I will give for the life of the world (John 6:48-51).

The Rescuer

Guard my life and rescue me;
let me not be put to shame,
for I take refuge in you.
PSALM 25:20

Upward Gaze

Father, You're worthy of praise, for You're my loving God and my fortress, my stronghold and deliverer, my shield in whom I take refuge (Psalm 144:2). You give victory to kings and delivered David from the sword (Psalm 144:10). I'll be glad and rejoice in Your love, for You saw my affliction and knew my soul's anguish (Psalm 31:7). Praise You, God! Amen.

"We're here," Jan said with a sigh to her husband, Larry, as they turned into the driveway of a friend's lakefront cabin. "I'm ready for a vacation."

Larry unlocked the cabin's door as Jan unbuckled three-year-old Michael's car seat. She watched her son race toward the house. *That boy's energy knows no bounds,* she thought. *He moves so fast—it's hard to keep up with him!* She lifted her sleeping infant from his seat and followed the toddler.

"This is perfect!" she said, stepping into the cabin. "No schedules. No phones. Just you and me and the kids." She grinned at Larry. "Life is good."

Larry returned her smile then glanced at his watch. "Hey—it's almost lunchtime. I'll unload the car."

Jan watched Michael follow his dad and then laid the baby on a bed. Within ten minutes she'd stashed groceries in the fridge and had begun preparing sandwiches. Larry searched the cupboards for plates and cups.

The sound of a boat's revving engine drew Jan's gaze outside. She froze—Michael was afloat on a five-foot by two-foot Styrofoam chunk far from shore! He'd gone exploring as his parents busied themselves with chores.

"It's Michael!" she screamed. Together the couple ran to the shore, where a canoe rested upside down. Larry flipped the boat, shoved it into the water, and paddled toward his son, whose makeshift raft was floating in water well over his head. The boy sat quietly on the foam, legs dangling in the water as he watched his dad approach.

When Jan recalls the incident, she says, "Michael sat still, quietly waiting for Larry. He didn't cry or scream or try to climb down. It was as though he knew that he should stay on that Styrofoam, that his dad would come for him sooner or later. He just had to wait."

Children often teach profound spiritual truths. Michael's story exemplifies how the Lord wants us to respond in difficult situations. God wants us to sit tight and wait confidently for Him to rescue us.

Three Old Testament teens displayed amazing certainty in God's ability to deliver them from a hot spot. They'd disobeyed King Nebuchadnezzar's commands to worship him. As a result, they found themselves staring into the mouth of a blazing furnace.

"Change your minds, or you'll be thrown into the furnace immediately!" the king shouted. "Then what god will be able to rescue you from my hand?"

How did the teens respond to the king's threats? In fear and panic? Did they shake their fists at God? Did they submit to the king to avoid the fire?

None of the above.

They answered, "If we are thrown into the blazing furnace, the God we serve is able to save us from it, and he will rescue us from your hand,

O king" (Daniel 3:17). They knew God could preserve them, and in faith, they stated that He would. And He did—in the midst of the flames.

God is the same today. He *can* and He *will* deliver us from difficult situations as He promised. Whatever we're facing today, we must wait with quiet confidence for our rescue. It may not come when we hope or in the way we think it should, but it will come.

And when others feel frightened or downhearted at their circumstances, we can encourage them with God's promises. We can direct their thoughts to the living God, pray with them for their rescue, and wait with them for the answer.

Inward Glimpse

Heavenly Father, thank You for delivering me from trouble. Help me wait in confidence for my rescue. Amen.

- How has God delivered you from a difficult situation in the past?
- Write a sentence or two in which you thank God that He's willing and able to rescue you.

Outward Glance

Father, I pray that You will rescue _____ because he loves You. Protect him because he acknowledges Your name. When he calls on You, please answer him. Be with him in trouble; deliver and honor him. Satisfy him with a long life and show him Your salvation (Psalm 91:14-16). Thank You. Amen.

One More Peek

Then Nebuchadnezzar said, "Praise be to the God of Shadrach, Meshach and Abednego, who has sent his angel and rescued his servants! They trusted in him and defied the king's command and were willing to give up their lives rather than serve or worship any god except their own God (Daniel 3:28).

Active Listening

*The eyes of the LORD are on the righteous
and his ears are attentive to their cry.*
PSALM 34:15

Upward Gaze

Heavenly Father, I praise You because Your eyes are on those who fear You, on those who hope in Your unfailing love (Psalm 33:18). You aren't like silver and gold idols made by men's hands. They have eyes but can't see and ears but can't hear (Psalm 115:3-6). But You are real—You hear my voice when I cry for help (Psalm 18:6). Amen.

MOM

"No one ever tells me anything!" Kim moaned again. "Why am I always the last one to hear about things?"

"That's not true," I corrected her. "You *were* told about our overnight guests. Twice."

She moaned once more for emphasis, then sought solitude in her bedroom.

I know I told her about the company, I thought. *Why does she say no one communicates with her?*

The next several weeks brought similar scenes. Finally the answer dawned on me. Although Kim heard people speak to her, she wasn't really listening to what they were saying. Instead, her thoughts focused on other matters—a math assignment, an upcoming volleyball tournament, or squeezing chores into her schedule.

At first I felt annoyed with her. *That's rude. I've trained her better than that.* Then the truth hit me. I *had* trained her. Yes, indeed, I was guilty of the same conduct.

Rather than listening, *really* listening to my kids when they studied at the kitchen table after school, I busied myself with household chores. Our conversation flew between the kitchen and wherever I happened to be working—the bathroom, our bedroom, the utility room, the living room. Most often my thoughts weren't on what they were saying at all. The proof came out later when they reminded me about plans they'd made with friends.

"What? When did you decide to do that? You need to tell me these things," I said more than once. "We did," they replied. "You weren't listening."

They were right. And I was missing out—not just on their schedules but also on their hearts, on what concerned them and brought them joy.

How can I fix this? I wondered. The answer came quickly—cease activity and look at my children's faces when they speak to me (except when I'm driving!). It made sense.

When I deliberately stop what I'm doing to engage my eyes and ears in communication, I'm less distracted and more able to absorb what my kids are telling me. My relationship with God works the same way.

I can learn much about spiritual listening skills from Jesus' visit to Martha's home. As she bustled about her kitchen preparing dinner, she caught conversation snippets from the other room, where He visited with His disciples and her sister, Mary. Her mind, however, wasn't focused on what she heard. Instead, she fussed and fumed about her workload.

Who does Mary think she is? Martha stewed. *Here I am, baking bread and grinding spices, and there she sits. A lot of help she is!* Finally she'd had enough. She marched into the front room, glared at Mary, and interrupted the conversation.

"Jesus, I'm a little overworked right now. Don't you care that my sister isn't helping?"

Jesus looked at her and smiled. "Martha, Martha, you're so busy with *things*, but only one matter is important. Mary has chosen what is better, and it can't be taken from her."

What was the better path Mary had chosen? Sitting in Jesus' presence, looking at His face, and listening, *really* listening to His words. As Mary ceased activity to communicate with the one who loved her unconditionally, she caught a glimpse of His heart—His passion for His Father and His love for mankind.

Her example doesn't give us the liberty to stop doing laundry and mending and vacuuming (wishful thinking...), but it teaches us the importance of setting aside distractions and practicing active listening. And the payback is worth the effort, for as we sit quietly in Jesus' presence, gazing into His face and listening to His voice, we'll understand more of His heart for people. We'll comprehend more about His perspective on life, and learn how to obey so others will see His likeness in us.

When we actively listen to our children, we'll understand *their* thoughts and hearts, too. And they'll capture a glimpse of how the Father cares for them.

Inward Glimpse

Dear Father, thank You for listening to me and hearing my voice. Help me set aside distractions and focus on You. Amen.

- On a scale of 1–10, with 10 being "totally attentive," how do you rate on listening to your children?
- How can you improve your skills?

Outward Glance

Father, I pray that _____ will see You with his eyes and hear You with his ears (Job 42:5). Thank You for promising to counsel him with Your eye upon him. May he be so focused on You that he hears Your instruction and teaching

(Psalm 32:8). And may he do what is right in Your sight (Deuteronomy 12:25). Amen.

One More Peek

Then a great and powerful wind tore the mountains apart and shattered the rocks before the Lord, but the Lord was not in the wind. After the wind there was an earthquake, but the Lord was not in the earthquake. After the earthquake came a fire, but the Lord was not in the fire. And after the fire came a gentle whisper (1 Kings 19:11-12).

Praise-Filled Mornings

It is good to praise the LORD
and make music to your name, O Most High,
to proclaim your love in the morning
and your faithfulness at night.
PSALM 92:1-2

Upward Gaze

Father, the heavens praise Your wonders and Your faithfulness, for no one compares with You (Psalm 89:5-6). I will sing of Your love forever. With my mouth I will make Your faithfulness known through all generations (Psalm 89:1). Amen.

‖ ‹MOM› ‖

Wake-up time hits our home sometime between 5:30 and 6:30 A.M. One early morning several months ago, I heard a faint, unfamiliar sound. *What's that?* I wondered.

I looked around our bedroom—the clock radio wasn't playing. I stepped into the living room—the CD player wasn't on. Curiosity drew me to the downstairs living area. The sound grew louder as I approached Stephanie's bedroom.

Strains of "Great Is Thy Faithfulness" filtered through her door. I stood outside, listening in awe as my teenage daughter celebrated God's goodness as she dressed for school. Several days later it happened again, then again.

Now it's routine, but I'll never grow weary of hearing her hum or sing God's praises. Her singing tells me she's happy to be alive and enjoying harmony with her Creator. Her day begins on a joyful note, and for that reason my heart sings, too.

Habitually beginning our day with praise transforms our perspective. Proclaiming God's loving-kindness each morning makes us less likely to whine about life's little hassles, such as traffic jams or spilled juice. We're less inclined to be fearful or anxious and more prone to practice contentment in all circumstances. Joy becomes our trademark, and its results affect those near us.

I witnessed an incredible example of this several years ago after three sisters, twins in their late teens and a sibling in her early twenties, joined our camp's spring staff. We enjoyed great talks about life—music, guys, college, friendships, and parents.

They enjoyed a close relationship with their folks. They specifically mentioned their mom's tradition of playing worship music early each morning. "Praise music is the first thing we hear when we walk downstairs for breakfast," said one. "It sets the tone for the whole day." They had no way of knowing that it had also prepared them for an unbelievably dark night.

One week after that conversation, a car accident claimed their mother. The girls rushed home for the funeral and then returned to pour their lives into summer campers for the next ten weeks. Heartwrenching grief couldn't squelch God-given joy.

Their mother's radiant relationship with Jesus Christ had evidenced itself through praise. She'd filled her home and her daughters' hearts with an understanding of God's love and faithfulness. As a result, the girls greeted death's dark night with calm assurance.

Of all mankind, believers have the most reasons to praise each morning! Just think—God loves us, guides our path, forgives our sins, protects and provides for us, promises eternal life, uses life's tough times for our good, and restores our souls when we're weary. His Word bears countless reasons for us to praise Him.

An attitude of praise transforms our faith. It lifts us from discouragement to delight as we focus on God and watch Him work. It changes our response from "I can't do this," to "I can hardly wait to see how God is going to do this!"

My prayer for you is that you will wake each morning with a song of praise in your heart and that it will spill into your home!

Inward Glimpse

Heavenly Father, thank You for giving me so many reasons to praise You. Tune my heart to sing Your praise. Amen.

- List three or four things for which you will praise God before rising each morning.
- Memorize today's verse. When you feel the blahs sneaking up, chase them away with the Word.

Outward Glance

Father, please make _____ glad by Your deeds. Teach her to sing for joy at the works of Your hands (Psalm 92:4). Teach her to praise You, for You are good. Put songs of praise in her mouth, for singing to Your name is lovely (Psalm 135:3). Amen.

One More Peek

Praise the LORD.
Praise the LORD from the heavens,
*   praise him in the heights above.*
Praise him, all his angels,
*   praise him, all his heavenly hosts.*
Praise him, sun and moon,
*   praise him, all you shining stars.*
Praise him, you highest heavens
*   and you waters above the skies.*
Let them praise the name of the LORD,
*   for he commanded and they were created*
*   (Psalm 148:1-5).*

Jump!

Surely God is my salvation;
I will trust and not be afraid.
The LORD, the LORD, is my strength and my song;
he has become my salvation.
ISAIAH 12:2

Upward Gaze

I will give thanks to You, Lord. I will make known among the nations what You have done and proclaim that Your name is exalted (Isaiah 12:4-5). Your word shows us that when You issue battle commands, You lead the way and accomplish the victory. We need not fear or be terrified, for You carry us like a child, just as You did Your people in Egypt (Deuteronomy 1:29-31). Amen.

When I was young, summer meant swimming lessons. Moms visited other moms on sun-drenched bleachers while their kids stroked and crawled for 30 minutes. At the end of the two-week session, the instructor barked, "Line up at the diving boards!"

"Yahoo!" daredevil boys cheered. They half-ran, half-walked to the pool's deep end, eager to out-splash rivals with their latest techniques.

My enthusiasm didn't match theirs. Diving boards intimidated me. Their side railings didn't extend far enough for my comfort. The boards bounced under my feet, threatening to spill me into water way over my head. And they were high. Dangerously high—at least to my nine-year-old imagination.

Perched on the diving board's tip, I shivered with fear.

"Jump!" the teacher called.

I couldn't. My legs wouldn't budge.

"You can do it!" he hollered again.

What was he thinking? Of course I couldn't! I backed toward the railing and then glanced over my shoulder. To my dismay, a boy had already climbed the ladder and was waiting for his turn. Another student paused halfway up the steps, and a half-dozen stood on the pool deck below him. All eyes focused on me.

Suddenly the teacher called, "I'll help you!" He entered the pool's deep end. "Jump! I'll be right here."

I looked at the water—it still seemed like a long, long way down. I looked at the teacher—he seemed so confident. I looked behind me—the kids were still there.

I plugged my nose, squeezed my eyes shut, and jumped, bobbing to the surface a split-second later. I was still alive! And my teacher was there to help, just as he'd promised.

At certain points along our spiritual journey, God asks us to jump. Often we respond by surveying the situation, cringing at the thought of leaping into the unknown, and shrinking back.

Perhaps we've been asked to teach a Sunday school class or women's Bible study, but we've never taught before and the thought unnerves us. Maybe outside employment demands more time than we can give without hurting our family, but curbing hours means cutting finances. Perhaps we've thought about extending friendship to our neighbors beyond "Hi, how are you?" but don't know how to do it. Maybe a teenage son or daughter senses God leading them into overseas missionary service, and we're hesitant to encourage them—*It's not safe. Besides, how will they raise missionary support?*

If God is clearly leading through circumstances, His Word, and the counsel of godly people, we can take the plunge without fear. We don't need to know all the details—they're His business. Our job is simply to obey.

Is jumping sometimes scary? Intimidating? Yup. How must the Israelites have felt when God commanded them to cross the flooding Jordan River? How did Noah feel when God directed him to build an ark? How might Abraham have felt when God instructed him to move his wife and household to an unknown new land?

Despite their fears or misgivings, these people obeyed. And God was with them. He's the same today. He issues a command, and His presence goes with us when we obey.

Inward Glimpse

Dear Father, thank You that Your presence goes with us when we follow Your commands. Remove my fear and teach me to trust. Amen.

- Recall an experience when God asked you to jump and trust Him. What happened?
- What frightens you about jumping into the spiritual unknown? Write out a Bible verse that counteracts your fear.

Outward Glance

Dear Father, as David prayed for his child, Solomon, so I pray for _____. I pray that he will be strong and courageous to do the work You've called him to do. May he not be afraid or discouraged but understand that You, the Lord, the mighty God, are with him. May he remember that You will not fail nor forsake him but will bring the work to completion (1 Chronicles 28:20). Amen.

One More Peek

See, the ark of the covenant of the Lord of all the earth will go into the Jordan ahead of you. Now then, choose twelve men from the tribes of Israel, one from each tribe. And as soon as the priests who carry the ark of the LORD—*the Lord of all the earth—set foot in the Jordan, its waters flowing downstream will be cut off and stand up in a heap* (Joshua 3:11-13).

The Way Maker

*Who among the gods is like you, O L*ORD*?*
Who is like you—
majestic in holiness, awesome in glory,
working wonders?
EXODUS 15:11

Upward Gaze

Father, You are highly exalted. You've hurled the horse and its rider into the sea. You are my strength and my song, and You have become my salvation. You are my God, and I will praise You (Exodus 15:1-2). Amen.

Heavy fog settled over our area recently, disrupting ferry schedules for several days. The ferry managed to deliver school kids from Quadra Island to Vancouver Island as usual until the morning the fog was thick enough to slice.

"Sorry," said the ferry employee at the terminal's entrance when I arrived with my daughters. "We're staying here until this fog lifts. You can wait and hope for the best, but you might wait all day." He shrugged apologetically.

The girls and I looked at each other and mentally weighed the options—sit all day in the line of vehicles just in case or go home. Either scenario meant missing school. "Let's go home," said Steph. Kim and I agreed.

We crept through the parking lot, searching for a place to turn around. Suddenly we saw about 30 men and women climbing a nearby ramp. "Hey!" said Kim. "The water taxi must be shuttling people back and forth from town."

She was right. The water taxi bobbed in the water, docked at a wharf below. Other passengers were already boarding, heading to town for work. "Let's go!" she exclaimed.

Stephanie and Kim plucked their way down the ramp and boarded the boat. Within minutes the aluminum vessel revved its motor and shoved off. "Thank you for making a way for the girls to get to school, Lord," I prayed as fog swallowed the boat.

Throughout the morning, several Bible stories came to mind. Each one illustrated God's ability to make a way through seemingly impossible circumstances. Imagine, for instance, the Israelites' terror as they stood on the Red Sea's banks. Waves splashed before them as the Egyptian army closed in from behind.

God loves impossible odds. In this case, He simply planted an angel between the Israelites and the Egyptians, and then He appeared in the form of a cloud. Throughout the night, the cloud brought darkness to one side and light to the other. At the same time, He delivered a strong wind and prepared a dry crossing through the sea.

In the morning, the Egyptians attacked. But as they chased the Israelites through the parted waters, God threw their ranks into confusion. He caused their chariot wheels to swerve and drowned the entire army.

We'll likely never face anything so dramatic, but we may face other situations that will feel equally daunting. Perhaps our teen feels the Lord directing him to a particular college. We'd love to encourage him to pursue his dreams, but the astronomical fees frighten us. A family emergency drains our savings. A serious illness strikes a loved one. An accident renders our spouse or child brain damaged.

We look at the circumstances and grimace. Maybe even cry. Maybe scream a little. And God looks down and says, as He did to Moses and the Israelites, "Why are you crying out to me? Tell the Israelites to move on. The Egyptians will know that I am the LORD when I gain glory through Pharaoh, his chariots and his horsemen" (Exodus 14:15,18). In other words, He receives glory when He makes a way where there seems to be no way, so we don't need to panic! He's up to something good.

God didn't lift the fog, allowing my daughters to cross on the ferry that morning. Instead, He made an unexpected way through it. Likewise, He might not change our circumstances, but He'll see us through.

Inward Glimpse

Father, thank You for making a way through impossible circumstances. Help me trust You in the face of overwhelming odds. Amen.

- How does today's "One More Peek" encourage you?
- Write Psalm 34:1 on a 3x5 card and memorize it. When you feel like you're facing the Red Sea and the Egyptians are fast approaching, recite it!

Outward Glance

Father, I pray that _____ will extol You at all times. May Your praise always be on his lips, especially when huge odds face him. May his soul boast in You, Lord, and may his faith encourage the disheartened. Please answer him when he seeks You, and deliver him from his fears (Psalm 34:1-2,4). Amen.

One More Peek

Do not be afraid. Stand firm and you will see the deliverance the LORD will bring you today. The Egyptians you see today you will never see again. The LORD will fight for you; you need only to be still (Exodus 14:13-14).

Rose-Colored Goggles

Rejoice in the Lord always.
I will say it again: Rejoice!
PHILIPPIANS 4:4

Upward Gaze

Among the gods there is none like You, Lord. No deeds can compare with Yours. All the nations will come and worship before You and bring glory to Your name. I will praise You with all my heart and glorify Your name forever. Great is Your love toward me. You're compassionate and gracious, slow to anger, abounding in love and faithfulness (Psalm 86:8-9,12,15). Amen.

Kim and her friend, Kristin, burst through the door. I did a double take as they bounded past me enroute to the bedroom. "Hey, girls!" I called. "What's on your faces?"

Kristin replied matter-of-factly, "Ski goggles." Without a moment's hesitation she continued, "They make the day look better." The girls scampered off to another adventure.

I laughed at their delightful creativity. Although rain clouds filled the sky, painting the landscape a gloomy shade of grey, the girls had thought of a way to cheer up their space wherever they went. Rose-colored goggles—a sure method to see life in a different light.

In his book *Who Put the Skunk in the Trunk?*, author Phil Callaway tells about two eight-year-olds' insight on life:

> The one asked the other, "Wouldn't you hate wearing glasses all the time?"
>
> The other responded, "Nope. Not if I had the kind Grandma wears. She sees how to fix lots of stuff, and she sees lots of cool things to do on rainy days, and she sees when folks are tired and sad, and what will make them feel better, and she always sees what you meant to do even if you haven't gotten things right just yet. I asked her one day how she could see that way, and she said it was the way she had learned to look at things when she got older. So it must be her glasses."[8]

Like the girls' goggles, Grandma's glasses have a way of turning a grey day into something beautiful. When the rain pours outside, Granny fills the house with the aroma of fresh-baked bread and thanks the Lord for watering the flower gardens. If a thunderstorm rolls in, she's reminded of God's mighty power. If a thrashing storm knocks out the electricity, she gives thanks for candles and curls up with a good book and an afghan.

I like Grandma's prescription. She sees whatever good can be squeezed from life's lemons, making mighty fine lemonade when others see only the rind. And what does she do with it? Shares that yummy lemonade with others. She wouldn't dream of hoarding it when others around her are parched and thirsty.

And Grandma's glasses aren't custom-prescribed for her alone. The rest of us can use them, too. How? By seeing life through God's Word. Our view is transformed by reading the Bible and applying its truth to our everyday lives.

Rather than focusing on hurts and disappointments, we can give thanks that Jesus understands our pain. When we're lonely, we can rejoice in the privilege of belonging to God's family. When life looks like a jumbled pile of puzzle pieces, we can walk in confidence and peace, knowing that our sovereign God sees the big picture and has an eternal purpose.

Practicing the truth of God's Word enables us to see beyond life's lemon rinds. And when we apply that truth, our attitude of trust and thanksgiving creates a thirst in those around us not yet walking in a personal relationship with Jesus Christ.

Inward Glimpse

Dear Father, open the eyes of my heart that I might view the ups and downs of life through the truth of Your Word. May my life create a spiritual thirst in the lives of those around me who don't recognize Your Word as truth. I ask this in Jesus' name. Amen.

- How do you tend to view life? Are there areas in which you need to get your prescription changed?
- Write a prayer to God, expressing your heart's desire to see life through His eyes.

Outward Glance

Father, I pray that _____ will live each day with a thankful heart, rejoicing in who You are (Philippians 4:4). May he lift up his soul to You every morning, choosing to acknowledge Your great love toward him, Your compassion and graciousness, Your faithfulness and mercy. Grant strength to him. Be his help and comfort. Let his enemies see You working on his behalf, and let them glorify Your name (Psalm 86:13,15-17). Amen.

One More Peek

Better is one day in your courts
than a thousand elsewhere;

I would rather be a doorkeeper in the house of my God
    than dwell in the tents of the wicked.
For the LORD God is a sun and shield;
    the LORD bestows favor and honor;
no good thing does he withhold
    from those whose walk is blameless.
O LORD Almighty,
    blessed is the man who trusts in you (Psalm 84:10-12).

Family Resemblance

Be imitators of God, therefore, as dearly loved children
and live a life of love, just as Christ loved us and
gave himself up for us as a fragrant offering and sacrifice to God.
EPHESIANS 5:1

Upward Gaze

You have done marvelous things, Lord. Your right hand and Your holy arm have made Your salvation known and revealed your righteousness to the ends of the earth (Psalm 98:1-3). The heavens proclaim Your righteousness, and all the peoples see Your glory! (Psalm 97:6). Amen.

MOM

Before our son, Matthew, left home to work with an international mission organization, he was required to attend a conference on the other side of Canada. He felt a little nervous because he wouldn't know anyone there, so I phoned a former colleague of mine who worked for that mission.

"Hey, Steve," I said. "Would you watch for Matthew? Introduce yourself to him. Maybe you could answer his questions."

"No problem," he answered. "What does he look like?"

"Just like his dad."

"I'll find him."

Sure enough, Steve picked Matt out from the crowd—a tall, blue-eyed blond with an easy smile like his dad's. The family resemblance made identification an easy task.

"I took one look at him and knew immediately whose son he was," Steve said later.

Two teenage friends, Alison and Kristin, also share a strong family resemblance with their parents. Physically, they inherited their dad's blond hair and their mom's brown eyes. Alison's laugh sounds just like her mom's. Their personalities also show similarities, for they received their folks' quick wit. When the girls spent a week with us recently, laughter pealed through the house. Several times I walked into the kitchen, half expecting to find their mom sitting at the table.

Even little people mirror their parents' personalities. Four-year-old Jordan displays a delightful sense of humor much like his mom and dad's. As he bounced around the house recently, his mom laughed and said, "You're so silly."

Jordan replied innocently, "It's not my fault!"

He was right. He has developed a sense of humor resembling his parents' because he spends his life with them. He has listened to their banter, heard their jokes, and caught their laughter. Now he mimics them.

The fact that our kids develop mannerisms or character qualities like ours carries both positive and negative ramifications! If we don't watch our tongues, our children will learn criticism and grumbling. If we repeatedly worry, become impatient, lose our tempers, or treat others disrespectfully, our sons and daughters will do likewise.

On the other hand, if we speak as Scripture commands, they'll learn praise and thanksgiving. If we model compassion to the needy or grieving, they'll learn to practice mercy. If we demonstrate hospitality to the lonely, they'll reach out to others, too. And when we see our kids replicate what we try to demonstrate, we experience pleasure.

Likewise, God the Father receives pleasure when we, His children, resemble Him. When we exemplify love, joy, peace, patience, kindness, goodness, faithfulness, gentleness, and self-control, others see Jesus Christ in us. We bear a spiritual family resemblance.

Developing Christlikeness takes time and discipline. It begins when we accept God's gift of salvation through Jesus Christ and place our faith in Him for eternal life. It grows as we spend time with our heavenly

Father, getting to know Him more intimately through His Word and quiet prayer times. It develops as we fellowship and worship with other believers. And it matures as we experience and endure difficulties.

My desire is to live my life so others can say, in the spiritual sense, "It's obvious whose daughter you are. You're just like your Father." I pray that this will be your desire, too.

Inward Glimpse

Heavenly Father, thank You for the privilege of being a part of Your family. Develop in me a spiritual family likeness that others cannot mistake. Amen.

- What positive qualities of yours do your children mirror?
- Write a note to each child, praising him for the Christ-like characteristics you see in his life.

Outward Glance

Father, I pray that _____ will live a life worthy of the calling she has received. May she resemble You as she walks in humility, gentleness, and patience, showing forbearance to others in love. May she be diligent to keep the unity of the Spirit in the bond of peace (Ephesians 4:1-3). Amen.

One More Peek

Those who belong to Christ Jesus have crucified the sinful nature with its passions and desires. Since we live by the Spirit, let us keep in step with the Spirit (Galatians 5:24-25).

Welcome to the Family

He predestined us to be adopted as his sons through Jesus Christ,
in accordance with his pleasure and will.
EPHESIANS 1:5

Upward Gaze

You are my Father, my Redeemer (Isaiah 63:16). Because Your unfailing love surrounds those who trust You, I will rejoice and be glad in You (Psalm 32:10-11). From heaven You look down and see all mankind; from Your dwelling place You watch over all who live on earth. Your eyes are on those who fear You, on those whose hope is in Your unfailing love (Psalm 33:13,18). Thank You for the privilege of being Your child! Amen.

◄ MOM ►

It was family camp talent night. Ten Skelding siblings trooped onstage and grinned at the audience. A moment later, they launched into a familiar song.

"Welcome to the family, we're glad that you have come to share your life with us and to grow in love," they chimed. The performance touched my heart, for every word rang true. Of the Skelding's fourteen children, adoption has welcomed nine.

Their revue deserved recognition not simply for the great vocals but also for what it represented—a family built on unconditional love and commitment. Those values were obvious in the way they related to each other during camp. For the most part they were each other's best buddies and personal cheering squad. Self-confidence and selflessness emanated from each boy and girl as they interacted with their siblings and other children.

Twelve-year-old Michael compares his life before and after becoming a part of this family unit. "My life was dark before, but now it's different," he says. "I have real brothers and sisters to play with, and a real mom and dad." His adoption gave him a second chance at life, and he's grateful.

Pam and John Skelding's role as adoptive parents accurately portrays God's fatherhood. The couple has willingly sacrificed time and finances to provide a loving home for needy children. They've committed themselves to provide for, teach, respect, discipline, and support each son and daughter for life. They've overlooked racial differences, accepted special needs, and modeled unconditional love. Their example has taught their kids to do the same. As a result, their family experiences unity and joy.

Scripture says that when we place our faith in Jesus Christ for eternal life, God adopts us as His children. He extends a universal invitation. Like the Skeldings, He embraces any skin color or physical need. When we join God's family, He commits to provide for, teach, protect, and support us.

Michael's reflection on his dark life prior to adoption carries deep significance. Scripture says that those who do not know God exist in darkness. Once they receive Jesus Christ as Savior, however, they walk in His light (1 Peter 2:9). Just as Michael feels accepted and loved in his physical family, believers enjoy brothers and sisters in God's family and a newfound relationship with their heavenly Father.

It's never too late to be adopted into God's family. To do that, we must recognize that we can't buy our way into His family with good works or a godly background, and we must acknowledge that we've broken His law and deserve the penalty for our sin. Then we ask Him to forgive us for our wrongdoings and thank Him for sending Jesus Christ to pay our penalty. When we place our faith in Jesus Christ for eternal life, the adoption papers are signed.

Once we're a part of God's family, we'll want others to join, too. We can extend an invitation by modeling God's unconditional love. Wise behavior, gentle words, and thoughtful deeds will whet people's appetites to taste the good life as part of the family of God.

Dear sisters, welcome to the family! I'm glad to share your life with you.

Inward Glimpse

Dear Father, thank You for adopting me into Your family. Help me model Your unconditional love and commitment to my children and to others in Your family. Amen.

- According to Romans 8:15-17 and Ephesians 1:14, what benefit do adopted children enjoy that slaves don't?

- Write a sentence or two of thanks to God for adopting you into His family.

Outward Glance

Father, I pray that _____ will understand her position as Your child. Help her comprehend what Your fatherhood means. Lavish the riches of Your grace on her, together with all wisdom and understanding. Make her life be to the praise of Your glory (Ephesians 1:7-8,12). Amen.

One More Peek

Those who are led by the Spirit of God are sons of God. For you did not receive a spirit that makes you a slave again to fear, but you received the Spirit of sonship. And by him we cry, "Abba, Father." The Spirit himself testifies with our spirit that we are God's children. Now if we are children, then we are heirs—heirs of God and co-heirs with Christ, if indeed we share in his sufferings in order that we may also share in his glory (Romans 8:14-17).

Count on Him

Yet he did not waver through unbelief regarding the promise of God,
but was strengthened in his faith and gave glory to God, being fully
persuaded that God had power to do what he had promised.
ROMANS 4:20-21

Upward Gaze

Father, there is no God like You in heaven above or on
earth below. You keep Your covenant of love with Your
servants who continue wholeheartedly in Your way. You made
a promise to David with Your mouth and fulfilled it with Your
hand (1 Kings 8:23-24). You'll do the same today. Amen.

Linda sat at her kitchen table with her open Bible. She read and
reread Psalm 113:9: "He settles the barren woman in her home as a
happy mother of children. Praise the LORD." *What is God saying to me?*
she wondered. *Perhaps He's promising good things to come. I can always*
hope. She tucked the verse in her heart and wrote the date in her Bible's
margin.

For the previous five or six years, Linda had tried unsuccessfully to
become pregnant. Her situation brought bitter disappointment each
time she watched other women proudly show off their new babies.
Mother's Day delivered quiet, personal grief, not flowers or cards.

Linda clung to the Scripture promise as she taught school and
enjoyed involvement in church activities. She watched three college

friends adopt children. She and her husband met a couple who had adopted an infant one month earlier; she became that child's godmother. Finally Linda and her husband decided to begin adoption proceedings. They filled out forms. Agencies interviewed them. They waited. And waited. Two years after they began the process, a counselor told them, "Thank you for applying with us. We'll contact you by letter at least once a year."

Linda cried all the way home. *How much longer will it be? Did God really give me a promise, or was my impression only wishful thinking?*

Five years passed before she received the life-changing phone call. "We have a baby girl for you!" said an agency representative.

On her daughter's first birthday, Linda read the Bible verse again. This time she noticed something new: "He settles the barren woman in her home as a happy mother of *children*."

Six months later, the phone rang again. This time the caller said, "Congratulations! You have a newborn son." With two babies to call her own, Linda had been settled in her home as a happy mother of children, just as God had said.

Linda remembers the years spent waiting and wondering, hoping and praying for a child. Through the ups and downs, she recalls the certainty of God's faithfulness. She had no idea how or when He would fulfill His word—that was up to Him. She simply prayed and believed.

Her example encourages *us* to believe God's promises, too. Because He cannot lie, He will do what He says He will do. However, sometimes He answers in ways we don't anticipate. Although Linda's promise brought a literal fulfillment, God used the same verse in a different way for another woman.

Margaret never bore physical sons or daughters, but as a result of founding our camp ministry with her husband a half century ago, hundreds and perhaps thousands of children follow Jesus Christ today. She is indeed a happy mother of children—spiritual children.

God's Word contains countless promises applicable to all mankind—forgiveness for sin, eternal life when we place our faith in Jesus Christ, His nonstop presence with us, strength to do what He's called us to do and more.

Sometimes He makes specific promises as He did for Linda. Don't be disheartened if you've received a promise but haven't seen its fulfillment. You may not see it happen in your lifetime. But rest assured, God will come through. Nothing can stop Him from doing what He says. Count on it. Thank Him for His faithfulness. Praise Him even before you see the fulfillment come to pass, and let Him show you what He's capable of doing!

Inward Glimpse

Dear Father, thank You for fulfilling Your promises. Help me trust You even if the answer takes a long time to arrive. Amen.

- God's Word contains many promises. Think of one that is particularly meaningful to you. What is its significance in your life?

- Write a prayer of thanks to God for keeping His promises. If you're waiting for the fulfillment of a specific promise, praise Him for keeping His Word even before you see it come to pass.

Outward Glance

Father, I pray that _____ will keep his confidence in You. May he persevere so that when he has done Your will, he will receive what You have promised (Hebrews 10:35-36). May his faith in You be strong, persevering through ups and downs because he sees You, the invisible one (Hebrews 11:27). Amen.

One More Peek

We want each of you to show this same diligence to the very end, in order to make your hope sure. We do not want you to become lazy, but to imitate those who through faith and patience inherit what has been promised (Hebrews 6:11-12).

Walking in Worship

For great is the LORD and most worthy of praise;
he is to be feared above all gods.
1 CHRONICLES 16:25

Upward Gaze

Father, I'll sing joyfully to You, for Your Word is right and true. You're faithful in all You do. You love righteousness and justice, and the whole earth is full of Your unfailing love (Psalm 33:3-5). You're resplendent with light, more majestic than mountains rich with game (Psalm 76:4). I will meditate on all Your works and consider all Your mighty deeds. Your ways, O God, are holy. No god is so great as You! (Psalm 77:12-13). Amen.

MOM

Aren't the verses in this prayer wonderful? They paint a magnificent description of God's character. They woo me to worship. I want to hide myself in a quiet place, kneel before God, and listen for His voice in the stillness. I want to draw apart from life's daily duties and devote undivided attention to the Person who loves me more than I will ever comprehend.

Some days, experiencing a worship time like this is possible. Other days, forget it. You know what I'm talking about. The phone rings, the dog barks, the kids squabble, the toilet plugs, the washing machine dances a jig across the utility room floor. Life's like that.

Routine responsibilities rob us of the luxury of lengthy solitude with God, but we don't have to be defeated. We can walk in worship in the midst of our activities—nursing babies, cooking dinner, driving kids to soccer games, folding laundry, or whatever. It *can* be done!

Several years ago, a friend introduced me to the book *The Practice of the Presence of God* by Brother Lawrence. It's a tiny book, a collection of thoughts gleaned more than 300 years ago while Brother Lawrence served in a French monastery.

One sentence in particular impacted me: "We should establish ourselves in a sense of God's presence by continually conversing with Him."[9] Making that statement one of my life's goals, I began training my mind to focus on the Lord at all times.

Menial tasks such as scrubbing floors and dusting have become a joy as I thank Him for my home and pray for my husband and children. Driving to the grocery store provides opportunities to pray for the families whose homes I pass. My morning shower is a time of thanking Him for the new day and committing it to Him. Many times throughout each day I recite Scripture to praise God for His mighty power, wisdom, and faithfulness.

After several years of practicing God's presence by conversing with Him, I've noticed a difference in my life. I experience peace and courage more often than worry and fear. Confidence in God's strength and wisdom has replaced insecurity and self-doubt. Joy and hope have replaced pessimistic thinking. My understanding of God's nature and character has deepened.

How about you? Does worry or fear haunt your thoughts? Has anxiety or life's busyness robbed your life of serenity and peace?

If so, you're not alone. We've all been there, but we don't have to stay there! We can ask the Lord to help us discipline our minds to focus on His character. We can talk with Him often throughout each day, telling Him He's wonderful, faithful, majestic, and holy! We can turn the mundane into opportunities for praise and worship as we practice the presence of God. By doing so, our spiritual lives will grow in ways we never thought possible!

Inward Glimpse

Heavenly Father, thank You that I can practice Your presence as I go about my day. Keep my thoughts on You and not the distractions around me. Amen.

- Write the words "Practice the Presence of God" on a 3x5 card and post it on your fridge as a reminder.
- Write a worship prayer to God. Begin with, "Heavenly Father, I praise You today because you are…." Perhaps you could tell Him what You appreciate most about His character and why: His faithfulness, unconditional love, power, holiness, wisdom….

Outward Glance

Holy Father, I ask that _____ will walk in Your ways and keep Your commands and laws so she may prosper in all she does and wherever she goes. May she watch how she lives and walk faithfully before You with all her heart and soul (1 Kings 2:3-4). May she delight in Your law and meditate on it day and night (Psalm 1:2). Amen.

One More Peek

Finally, brothers, whatever is true, whatever is noble, whatever is right, whatever is pure, whatever is lovely, whatever is admirable—if anything is excellent or praiseworthy—think about such things. Whatever you have learned or received or heard from me, or seen in me—put it into practice. And the God of peace will be with you (Philippians 4:8-9).

God's Economy

I know that you can do all things;
no plan of yours can be thwarted.
JOB 42:2

Upward Gaze

Heavenly Father, I praise You because You have established Your throne in heaven, and Your kingdom rules over all. From everlasting to everlasting, Your love is with those who fear You and Your righteousness with their children's children, with those who keep Your covenant and remember to obey Your precepts (Psalm 103:17-19). Amen.

MOM

While in Nepal, we watched men and women weave oriental rugs. Sitting at a loom several feet wide, each individual created an intricate pattern using strands of dyed wool. They blended rich shades of blues, reds, and greens with black, browns, or white to form original floral or abstract designs. They strategically placed each colored yarn as an integral part of the project. Workers wasted neither yarn nor energy in their efforts to produce a stunning product.

That scenario reminds me of the way God twists together various experiences, positive and negative alike, to accomplish His purposes in our lives. Nothing is wasted in His economy.

About a year after we moved to British Columbia, we heard that Operation Mobilization's oceangoing bookstore, the *Logos II*, was scheduled to dock in Nanaimo, a port about two hours from our home. Even though I'd never seen the ship, I'd heard about it for years because nearly 20 years earlier, I'd attended church with a young couple who later joined its staff. The fellow was now the ship's director and lived aboard with his family.

"Let's e-mail Myles and Patty," I said to Gene one day. "Perhaps we can meet them for lunch and take a tour of the ship." That's exactly what happened. After eating lunch in the vessel's dining room, Myles gave us a complete tour, including the engine room and their family's personal living quarters.

When our visit ended, Myles gave Matthew a book about the ship's history and worldwide ministry. Matt, an avid reader, devoured it within a day or two and then turned his focus back to his school studies and a favorite activity, playing trumpet in jazz band.

He worked hard throughout high school, hoping to win scholarships to attend a Christian university several hours from home. His grades consistently fell in the high nineties. We felt confident that scholarships would help pay his way through university.

Things didn't happen as we'd hoped. One by one, his applications were rejected. "What are you doing, God?" Gene, Matthew, and I asked many times. We finally realized that He held other plans.

What were they? He wanted Matt aboard the *Logos II*, working in the engine room and playing his trumpet in a worship band.

God took various experiences and wove them together to accomplish His purposes for Matt's life. Nothing was wasted in God's economy, including my friendship with Myles and Patty 20 years earlier, the vessel's first visit to Nanaimo after we moved to a nearby island, Matt's trumpet playing ability, the tour of the complete ship, the book Matt received, and the scholarship rejections. Each yarn helped complete the overall design.

God is all-knowing, all-powerful, and full of loving-kindness, so He uses whatever circumstances we face to achieve what He knows is best for us and for His glory. If we allow Him, He uses not only our strengths and victories but also our weaknesses, disappointments, and failures to produce the results He wants.

That knowledge doesn't give us the liberty to do whatever we please in the hopes that God will redeem it in the end. It does, however, grant us freedom from worry and fear. It give us confidence that God wastes nothing as He intertwines countless personal experiences and relationships to produce the big picture—the image of Jesus in our lives.

Inward Glimpse

Dear Father, thank You for blending circumstances together in my life to make a beautiful picture. Help me rest as You work in my life. Amen.

- How have you seen God weave assorted circumstances or relationships together in your life for your good and His glory?
- Read Joseph's story in Genesis 37 and 39–45. Take your time—you might need a couple of days so you don't feel rushed. Joseph's life bears amazing witness to the fact that God masterfully weaves circumstances for His highest purpose. List several situations that show God's sovereignty in Joseph's life.

Outward Glance

Father, I pray that _____ will fear You. May she enter into the great goodness You have for her (Psalm 31:19). I pray that she will place her confidence in You. As she does, please make her like a tree planted by the water that sends out its roots by the stream. May she not fear or worry in times of heat and drought, and may she always be fruitful (Jeremiah 17:7-8). Amen.

One More Peek

But God sent me ahead of you to preserve for you a remnant on earth and to save your lives by a great deliverance. So then, it was not you who sent me here, but God....You intended to harm me, but God intended it for good to accomplish what is now being done, the saving of many lives (Genesis 45:7-8; 50:20).

Steadfast, Immovable

"Though the mountains be shaken and the hills be removed, yet my unfailing love for you will not be shaken nor my covenant of peace be removed," says the LORD, who has compassion on you.
ISAIAH 54:10

Upward Gaze

Father, because of Your great love we are not consumed, for Your compassions never fail. They are new every morning. Your faithfulness is great (Lamentations 3:22-23). Those who trust You will go out in joy and be led forth in peace; the mountains and hills will burst into song before them, and all the trees of the field will clap their hands (Isaiah 55:12). Amen.

◄ MOM ►

Betty pulled a steaming casserole from the oven. *Only ten dinners left in this house,* she thought. *Hard to believe we're moving so soon.* She set the dish on the counter and looked around her kitchen, the scene of countless warm memories—Christmas celebrations and informal potlucks with family and friends, heart-to-hearts with her husband after tucking the kids into bed, board games with the children around the table. *I'm not so sure I'm ready for this,* she thought. *And what about the kids? They're doing so well right now. Why in the world are we ripping them from established friendships and routines?*

Shake it off, Betty, she chided herself. *You know this is a good thing. It's meant to be.* She recalled the circumstances leading to their move—their desire for a change, her husband's successful interview and subsequent new job, the sale of their house less than two days after putting it on the market, finding a more-than-adequate house in the new city. Details had come together quickly and had been pain free. Well, relatively pain free. Until now, that is. Her husband's job had required his immediate relocation, leaving her alone with the kids to say their goodbyes and mentally process the transition.

It was tougher than Betty had anticipated. Her neighbor reported that Holly had said she loved the new house and could hardly wait to move. At home, however, Betty received a different message. She recalled her daughter's outburst after school that day: "I don't want some little kid sleeping in my bedroom and touching my windows! I don't want him playing on my slide and learning to walk in the same house where I learned to walk!"

Matthew seemed to be handling it more positively. He anticipated setting up his new room, attending a different school, and participating in a church youth group. Despite his ability to look ahead, however, Betty knew he dreaded saying goodbye to his best friend. The boys had started school together, sharing numerous adventures and jokes over the years. The move meant splitting them up, robbing them of future good times. It didn't seem right.

In the midst of worrying about the kids' adjustment, Betty faced her own emotional upheaval. She found herself torn between anticipating an exciting, uncharted future and clinging to the comfortable past. *Why is this so hard?* she wondered.

She recalled a friend's recent words: "Like gold, we all look good on the outside. But the refining fire's heat reveals impurities and brings them to the surface."

That's for sure, Betty thought. *I thought I knew what it meant to trust the Lord, but this situation has revealed otherwise.* Feeling overwhelmed, she asked several friends to pray for her family.

"Changing circumstances can't alter God's faithfulness," they reminded her. "Temporary instability can't reduce His steadfastness."

Their insight holds true in all situations, even the most uncertain. We all want encouragement, especially in light of today's unsettling news headlines, but we must seek stability in an unchanging source. God's Word tells us that His faithfulness never changes even though everything around us shakes and totters. Finances, health, personal relationships—all can instantly change. But true to His Word, God remains steadfast, immovable. When we seek refuge in Him, His Holy Spirit reassures us that we are safe.

When changing circumstances surround you, may you find stability in the immovable, unchanging God!

Inward Glimpse

Dear Father, thank You for being steadfast in the midst of changing circumstances. Help me rest in Your constancy. Amen.

- What changing circumstances are you facing today? What concerns you most?
- Write a prayer and commit those concerns to the Lord. Thank Him that He's able to see you through.

Outward Gaze

Heavenly Father, I pray that _____ will keep his mind steadfast. May he trust in You at all times and know Your perfect peace. I pray that he will know you as the Lord, the Rock eternal (Isaiah 26:3-4). Amen.

One More Peek

God is our refuge and strength,
an ever-present help in trouble.
Therefore we will not fear, though the earth give way
and the mountains fall into the heart of the sea,
though its waters roar and foam
and the mountains quake with their surging
(Psalm 46:1-3).

God's Love and Cooked Spaghetti

Give thanks to the LORD, for he is good;
his love endures forever.
1 CHRONICLES 16:34

Upward Gaze

Heavenly Father, Your love reaches to the heavens, Your faithfulness to the skies (Psalm 36:5). I trust in Your unfailing love. My heart rejoices in Your salvation. I will sing to You, for you have been good to me (Psalm 13:5-6). Be exalted, O God, above the heavens; let Your glory be over all the earth (Psalm 57:11). Amen.

MOM

"What should we cook for Dad's supper?" I asked my sister, Joyce, as I flipped through Mom's recipe file.

"Spaghetti!"

"Mmmm. Sounds good! You cook the sauce. I'll boil the noodles. We'll surprise him." Mom's weeklong absence had left Joyce and me, ages 15 and 12 respectively, responsible for cooking Dad's meals. We enjoyed the independence.

"We're almost ready!" I told Dad when he came home from work. "We cooked noodles. All we have to do is drain them and then you can eat."

The pot and its contents weighed too much for me to manage alone, so I recruited Joyce's help. She held and tipped; I adjusted the lid to drain the water. That's when it happened.

The lid slipped! I jerked my hand to escape the steam, but in doing so, I yanked the lid off the pot. Cooked spaghetti plopped into the stainless steel sink and slithered down the garbage disposal. Frantic efforts rescued a handful of noodles—barely enough for one person, certainly not enough for three.

"Rats!" I cried. "We were soooo close to being ready. Now we have to start all over." I glanced at Dad, who smiled and shrugged. "It's okay," he answered. "I'll wait for the next batch."

How easily Dad, hungry after a long day's work, could have exploded when his meal vanished! Instead, he uttered no harsh words or criticisms. No commands to "hurry it up!" And even though spaghetti wasn't one of his favorite meals, he expressed an appreciative "thanks for cooking supper." Best of all, he continued to love me despite my botched effort.

I didn't realize it then, but as an adult I understand that Dad's response reflected the heavenly Father's heart for His daughters. Sometimes we try so hard to please Him, but our best efforts fall flat. How does He respond—does He throw a fit? Does He berate us with name-calling?

Absolutely not. Our heavenly Father looks beyond the fumbles, sees our heart's desire to please Him, and keeps on loving us. This has proven true many times in my life. For instance, I recall trying to sing a duet with a friend at a firefighters' Christmas banquet. We'd chosen "Silent Night" because we believed it conveyed the season's true meaning and hoped its message might challenge the listeners to ponder their need for Christ the Savior.

My friend strummed an introduction on her guitar and we launched into our well-rehearsed song. At that exact instant, stage fright gripped me. Missing my first note, I struggled to find the next. No luck. A restart yielded similar results. A third attempt nearly ended in disaster, too. By that time, I felt totally humiliated. Like cooked spaghetti noodles, my best efforts slipped down the drain and dragged my ego along. Did God stop loving me? Not a chance.

Fumbles happen. But when they do, our heavenly Father's love for us remains the same. He scoops us into His arms and says, "It's okay. I know your heart. I won't turn my back on you over this."

Sometimes fathers, or mothers for that matter, don't display God's grace when their children make honest blunders. If you've experienced someone's unwarranted wrath, I pray that God will heal your hurts and bring you into a clearer understanding of His unfailing love.

And I pray that we, as moms, will reflect God's never-ending love to our children when their best efforts fail. May we pick them up, brush them off, and send them on their way with a kiss and a prayer, encouraged to try again.

Inward Glimpse

Heavenly Father, thank You for loving me even when I fumble. Help me show Your unconditional love to my children when their best efforts fall flat. Amen.

- Can you recall a time when you tried hard but failed? How did you feel? If you're still hurting from that experience, write a prayer of thanks to God that He still loves you. If you've moved beyond that incident, thank Him for that same unconditional love.

- Write a note to each of your children, assuring them of your unconditional love. If they're too young to read, draw a picture of a mom and child holding hands and draw a heart around them. Color it with them.

Outward Glance

Father, thank You for loving _____ unconditionally. When she faces failures and disappointments, may she trust in You. Through Your unfailing love, may she not be shaken (Psalm 21:7). Keep Your love ever before her, and may she walk continually in Your truth (Psalm 26:3). Amen.

One More Peek

You are forgiving and good, O Lord,
  abounding in love to all who call to you.
Teach me your way, O LORD,
  and I will walk in your truth;
give me an undivided heart,
  that I may fear your name.
I will praise you, O Lord my God, with all my heart;
  I will glorify your name forever.
For great is your love toward me;
  you have delivered me from the depths of the grave
  (Psalm 86:5,11-13).

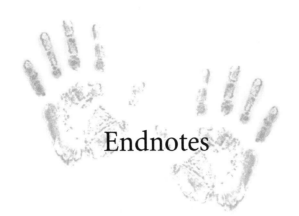

Endnotes

1. Phil Callaway, *Who Put My Life on Fast Forward?* (Eugene, OR: Harvest House, 2002), p. 126.

2. Phillip Keller, *A Shepherd Looks at Psalm 23* (Grand Rapids, MI: Zondervan Publishing House, 1979), p. 21.

3. Oswald Chambers, *My Utmost for His Highest* (New York: Dodd, Mead, and Company, Inc., 1935), p. 237.

4. Myrna Alexander, *Behold Your God* (Grand Rapids, MI: Zondervan Publishing House, 1980), p. 99.

5. Oswald Chambers, *My Utmost for His Highest* (New York: Dodd, Mead, and Company, Inc., 1935), p. 259.

6. J.I. Packer, *Knowing God* (Great Britain: Hodder and Stoughton Limited, 1975), p. 87.

7. Dr. Gary Smalley, *The Amazing Connection Between Food and Love* (Wheaton, IL: Tyndale House Publishers, 2001), pp. 41, 50.

8. Phil Callaway, *Who Put the Skunk in the Trunk?* (Sisters, OR: Multnomah Publishers Inc., 1999), p. 153.

9. Brother Lawrence, *The Practice of the Presence of God* (Uhrichsville: Barbour and Company, Inc., 1993), p. 12.

More Books You Can Believe In™
from Harvest House Publishers

15 Minutes Alone with God
Emilie Barnes

A devotional for every busy woman who finds it hard to squeeze in a consistent "quiet time" and Bible reading. Each devotional takes 15 minutes or less and contains a key verse, an uplifting meditation, and several "Thoughts for Action."

Minute Meditations™ for Busy Moms
Emilie Barnes

Time-challenged moms get encouragement and discretion for reflecting Christ in their homes and beyond. Short prayers and action steps help readers put challenging notions into motion. A prayerful pick-me-up for mothers on the go.

5-Minute Retreats for Moms
Sue Augustine

For the second book of this highly successful series, Sue Augustine has created dozens of creative ways moms can take a few pleasurable moments for themselves without the guilt that will rejuvenate their minds as well as the spirits.

Where Are You, God?
Michelle McKinney Hammond

Michelle's powerful meditations illustrate God's readiness to help people in times of loneliness and struggle. Using examples from the Bible—Daniel's standing alone for God, Thomas' time of doubting—these devotions encourage and uplift.